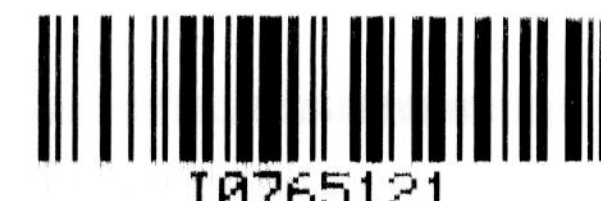

THIS BOOK BELONG TO ......

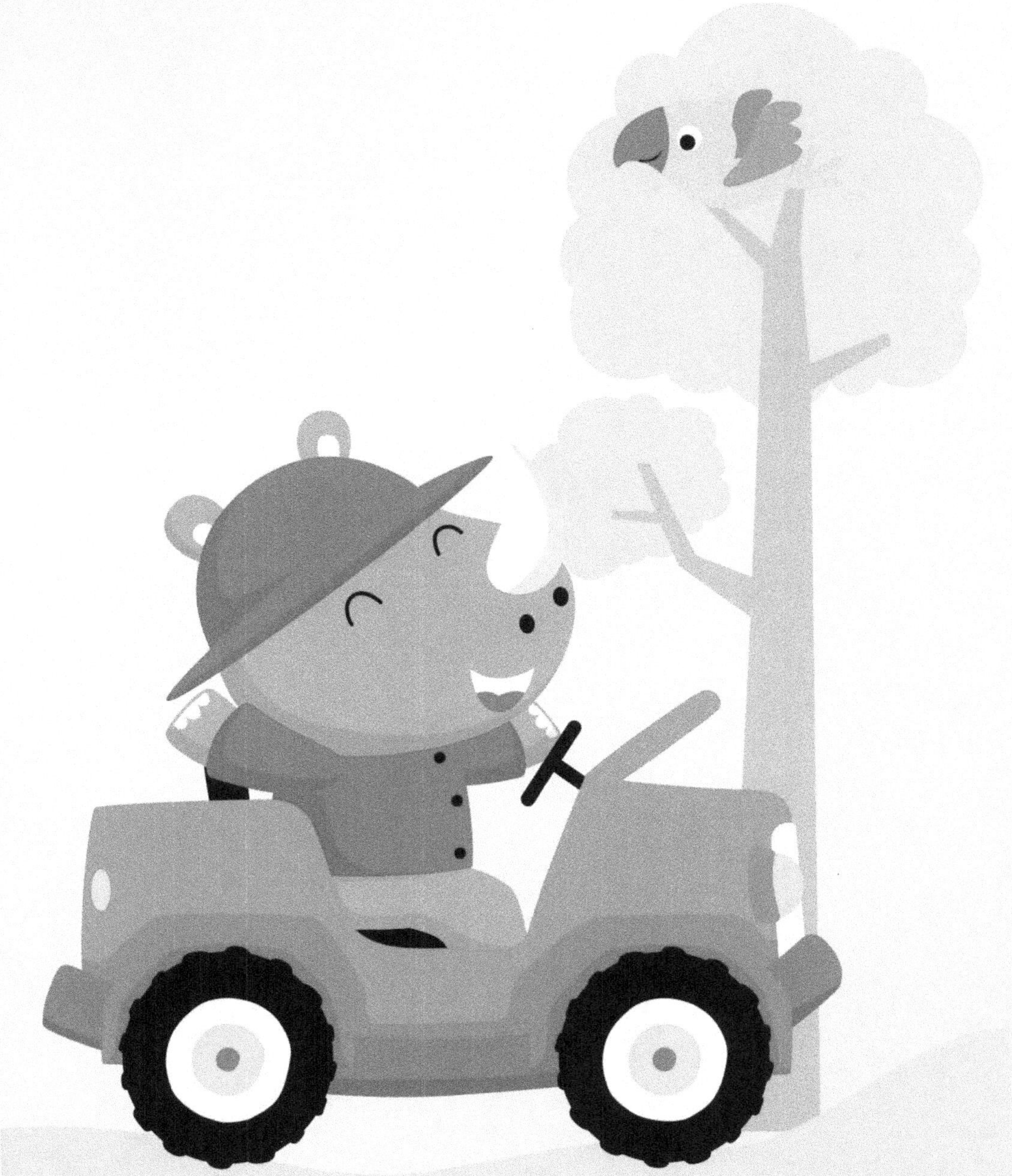

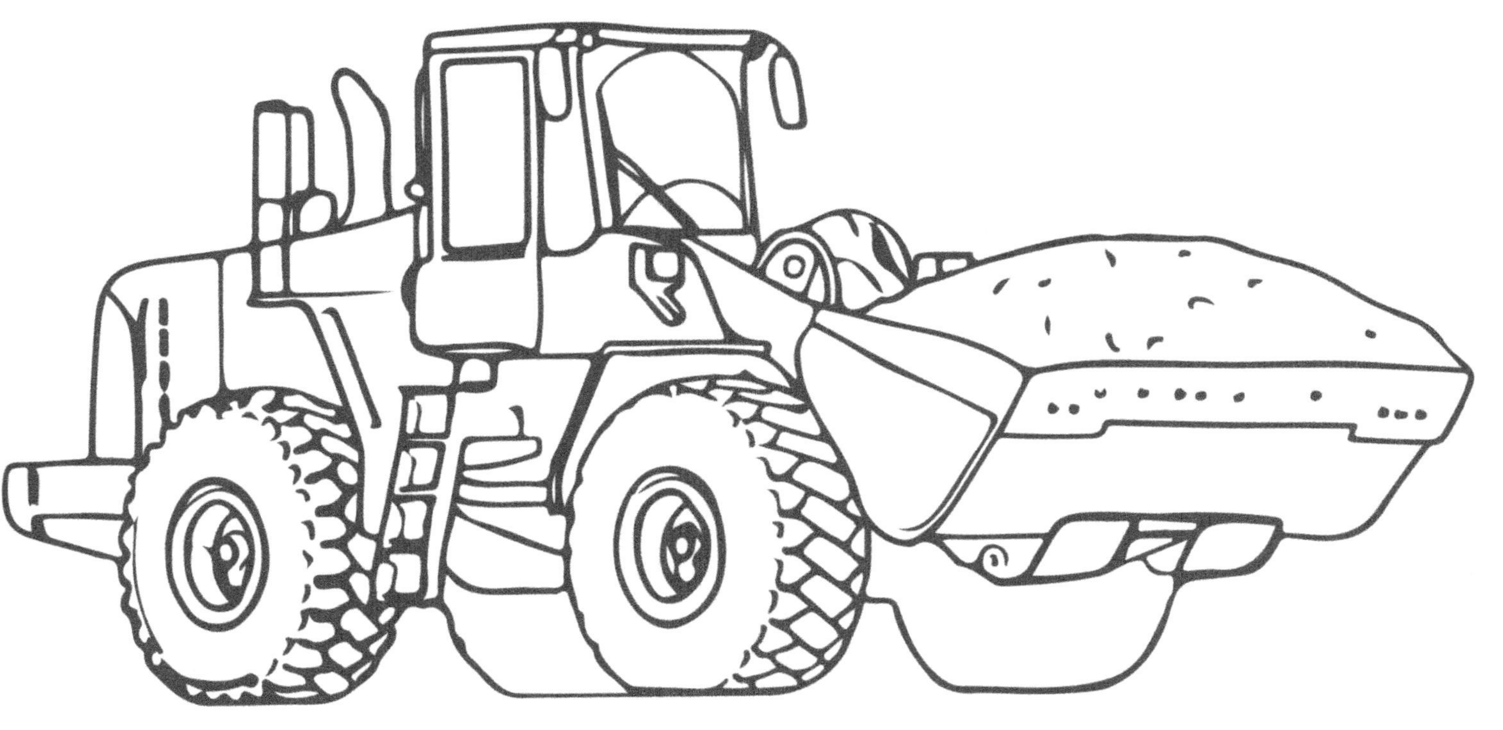

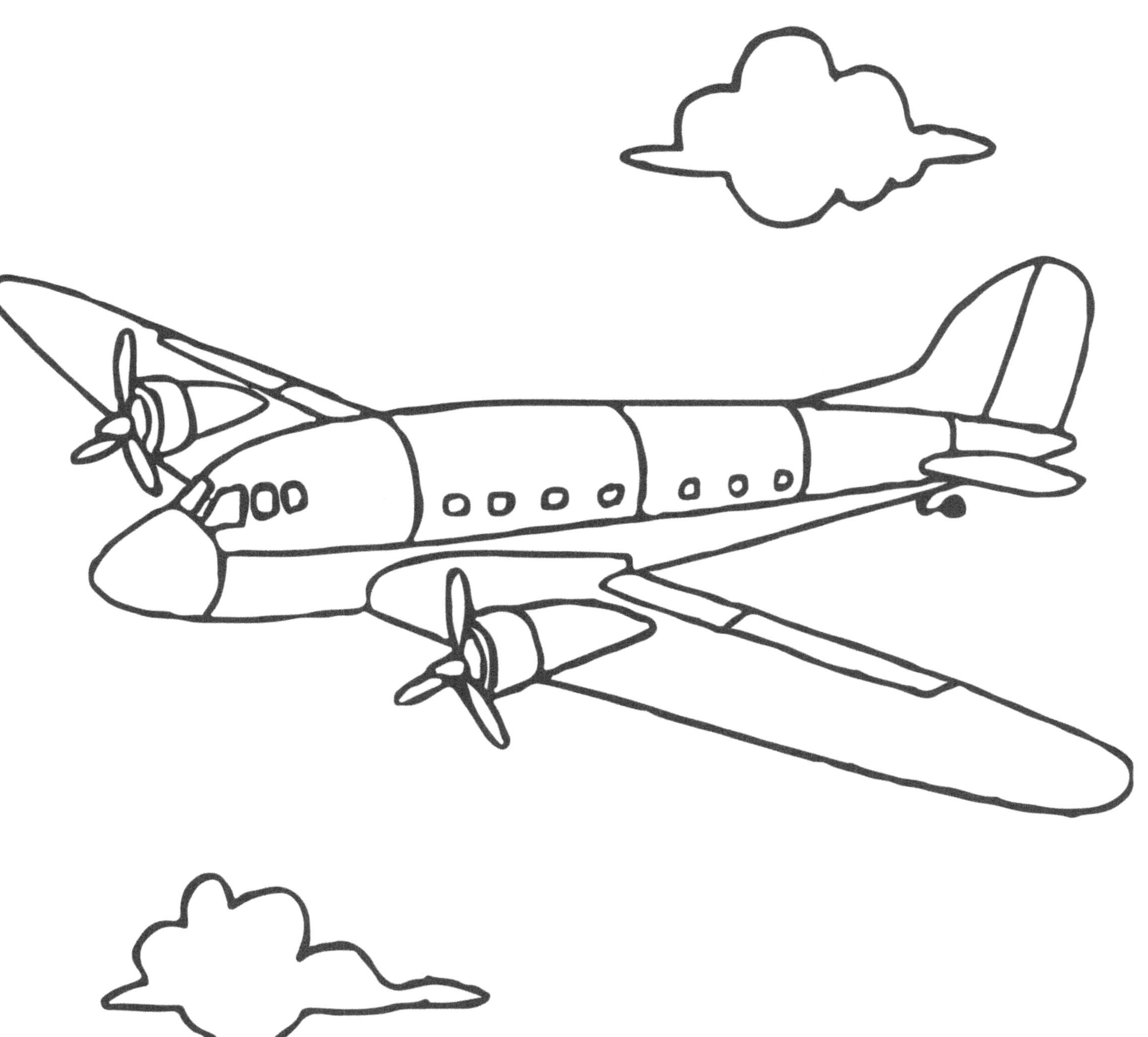

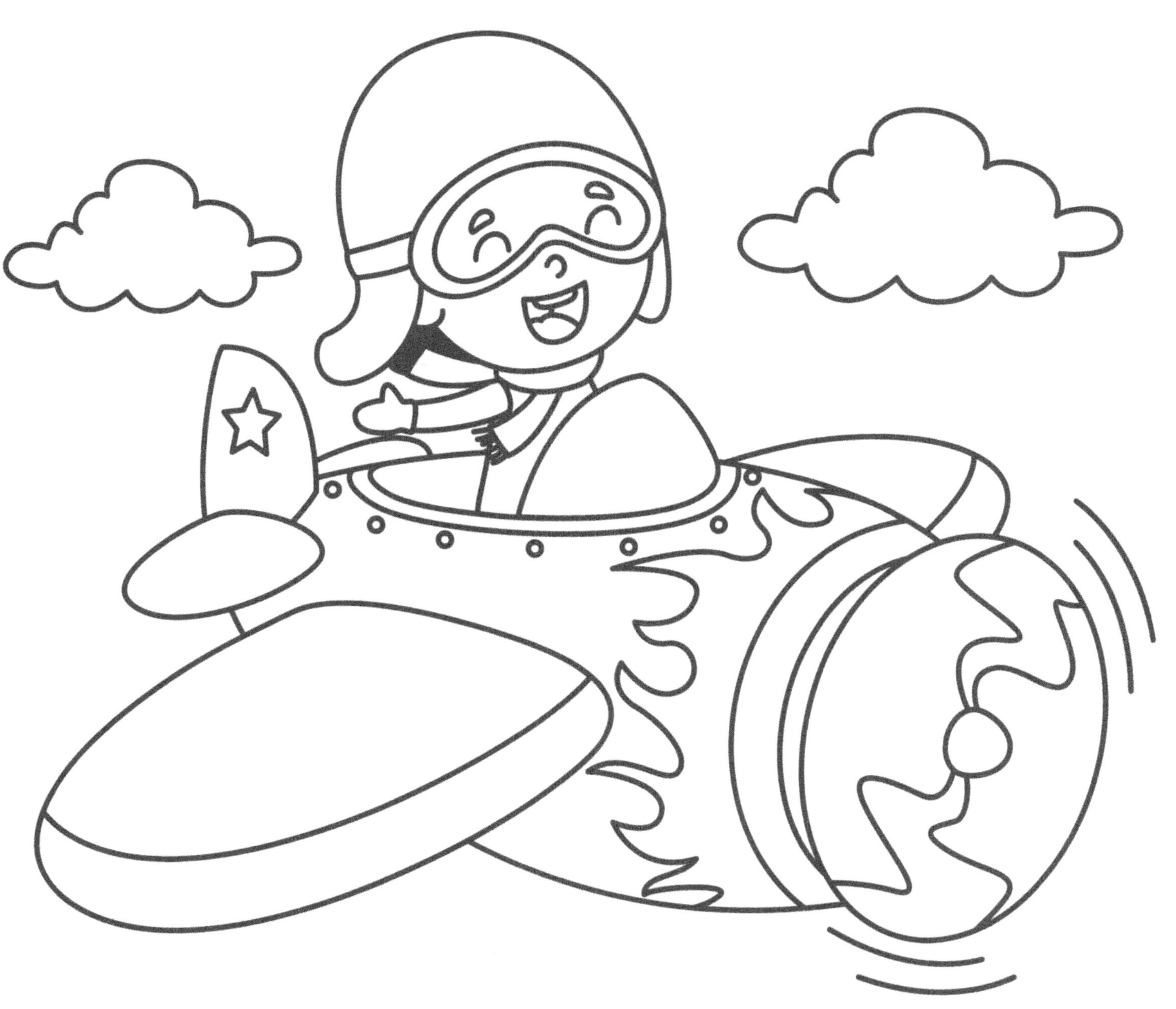

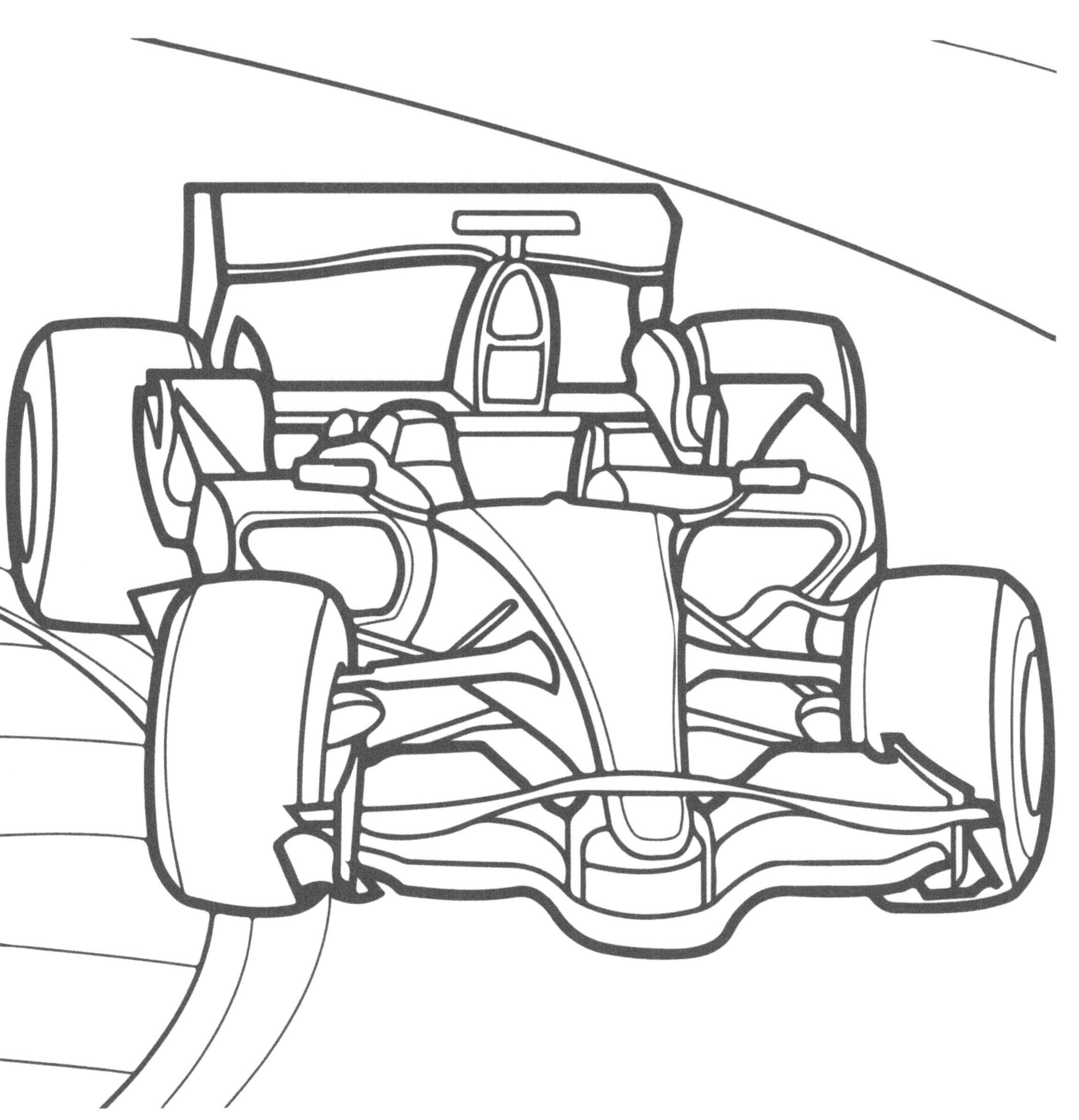

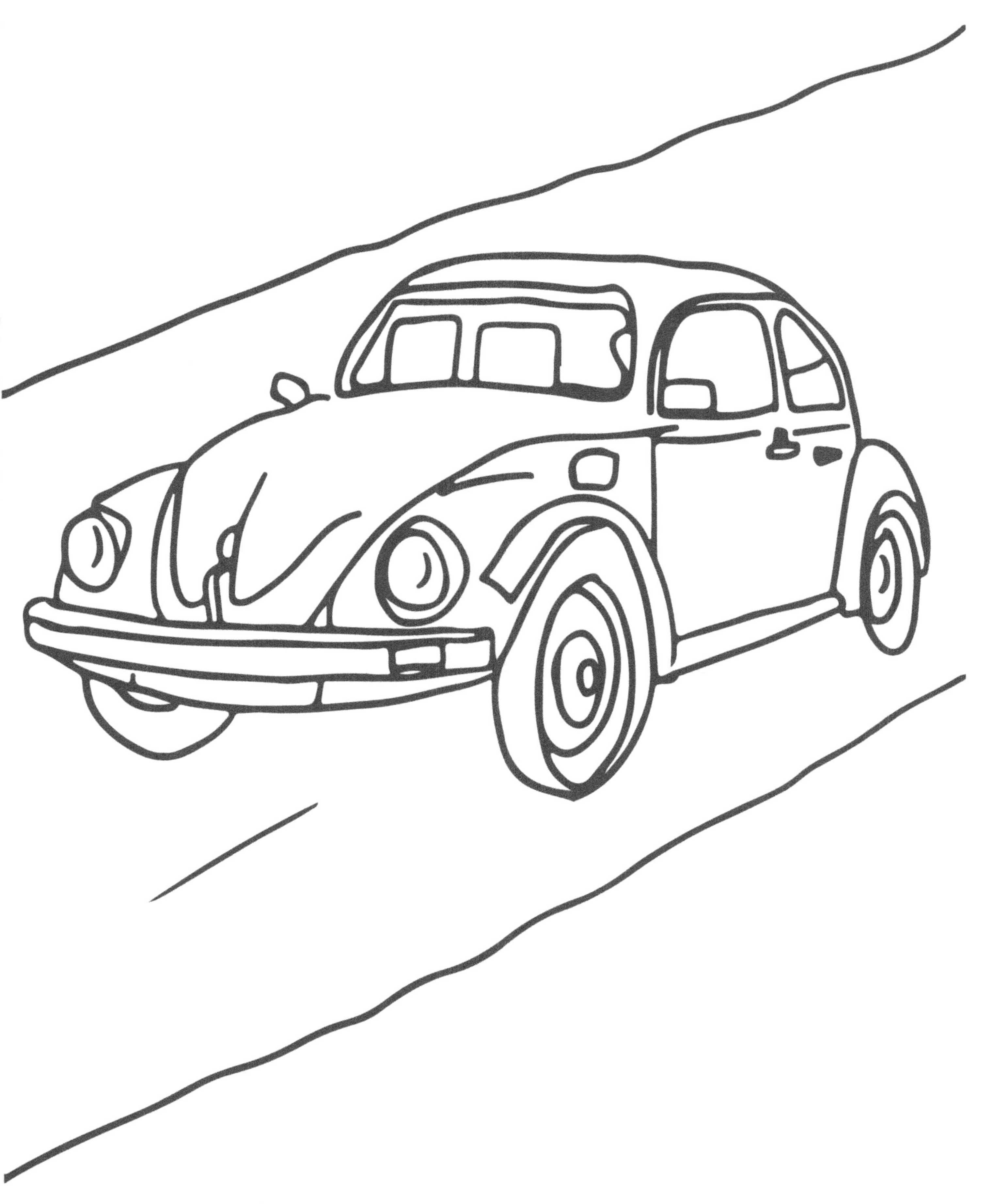

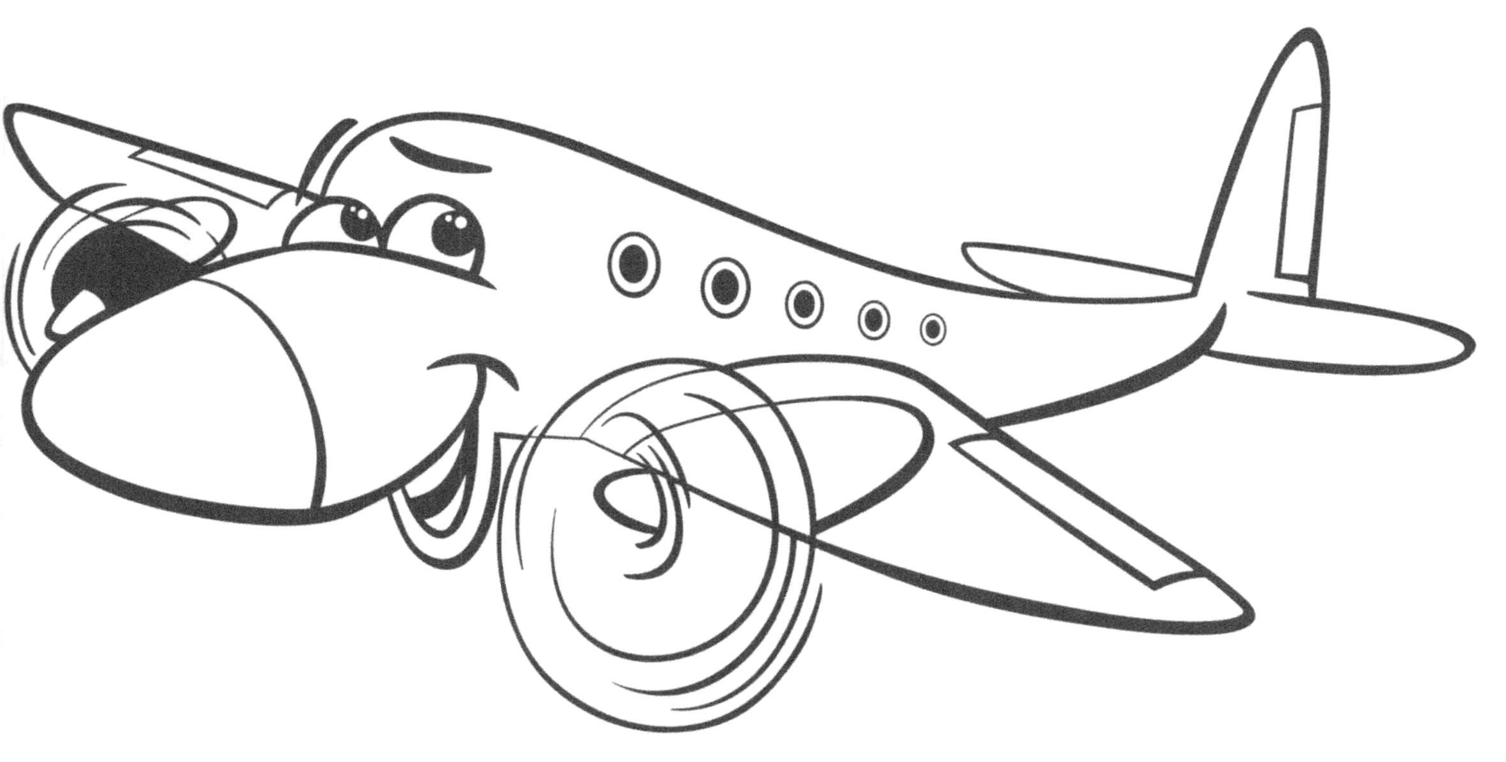

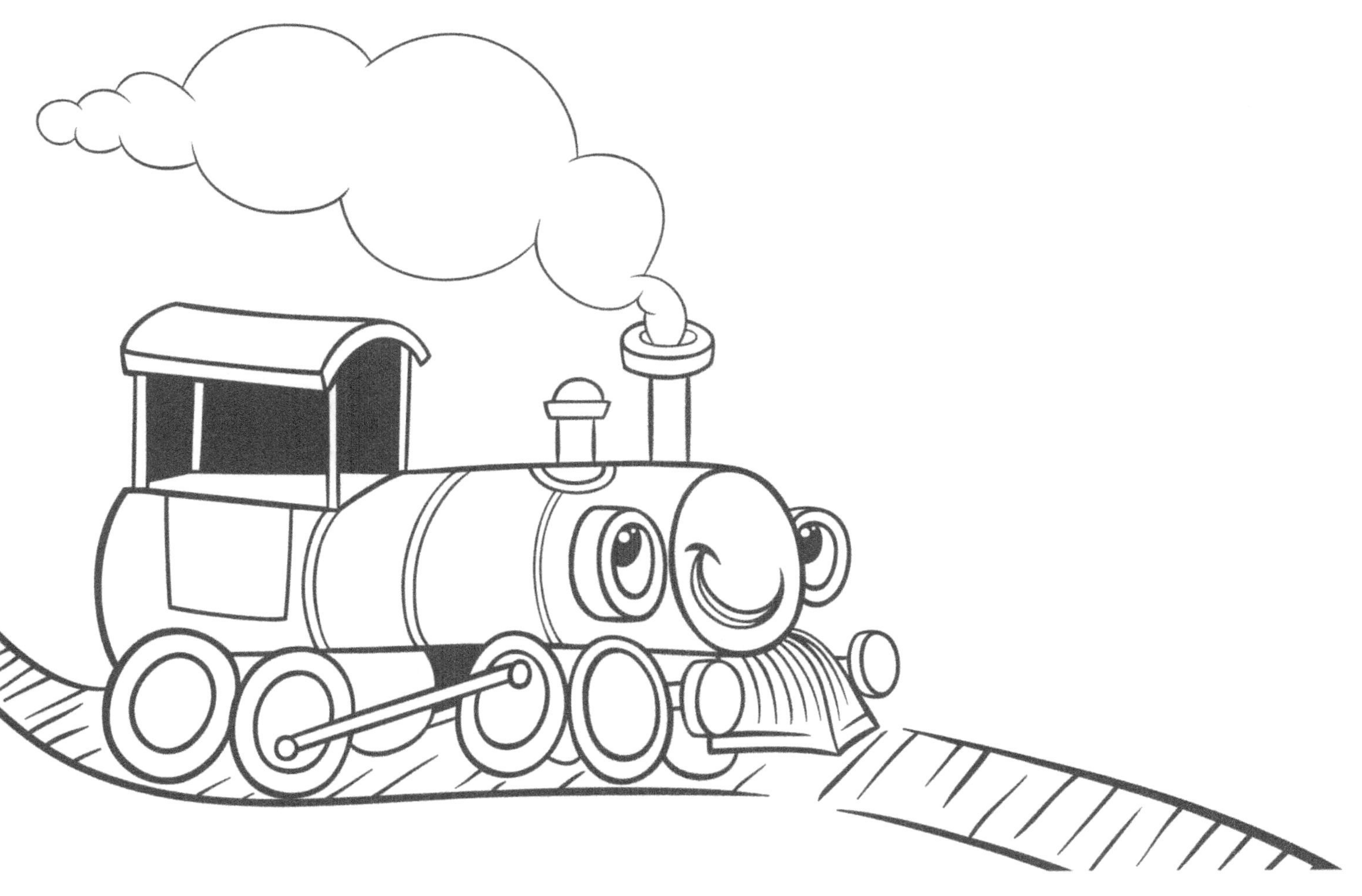

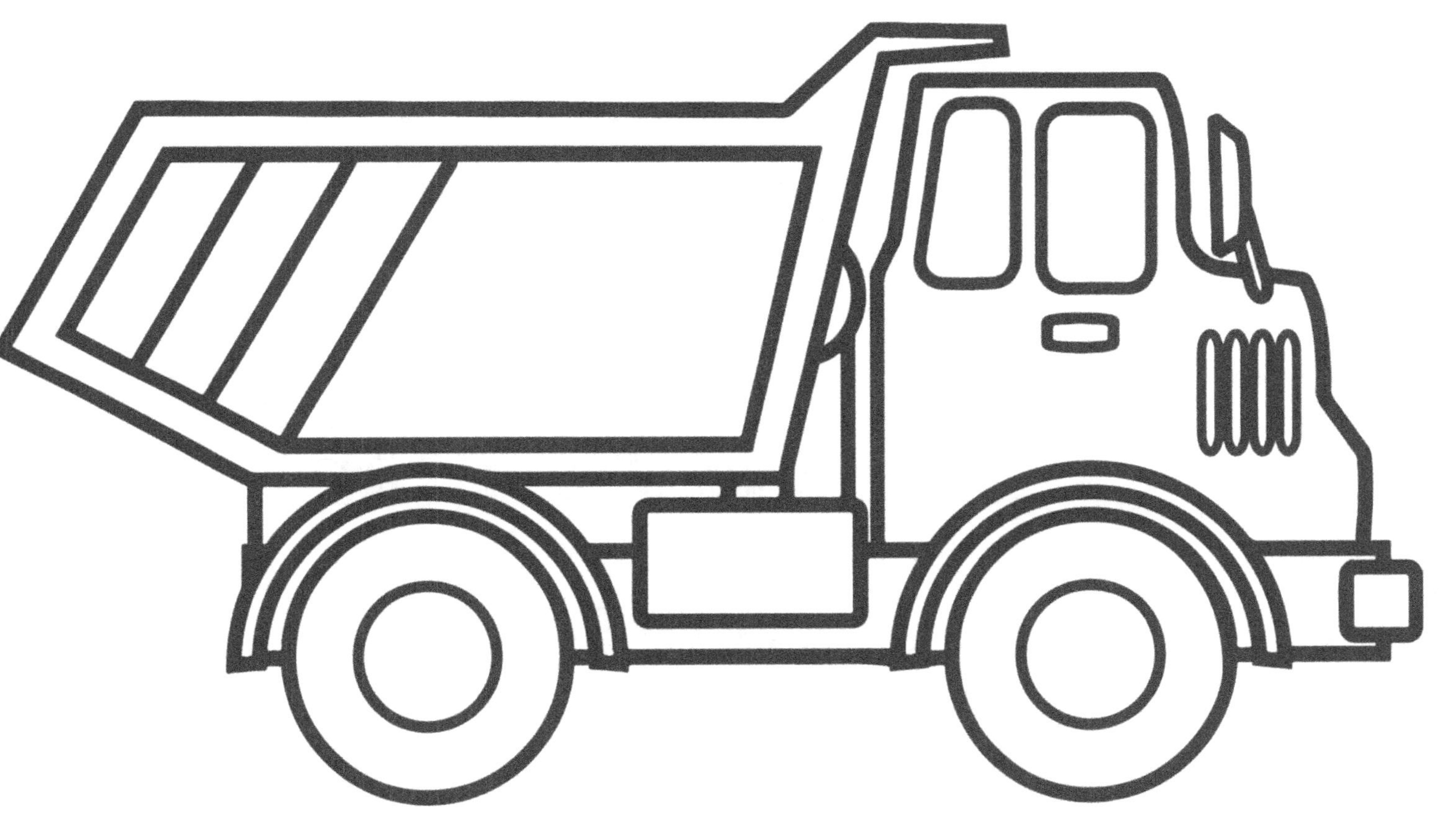

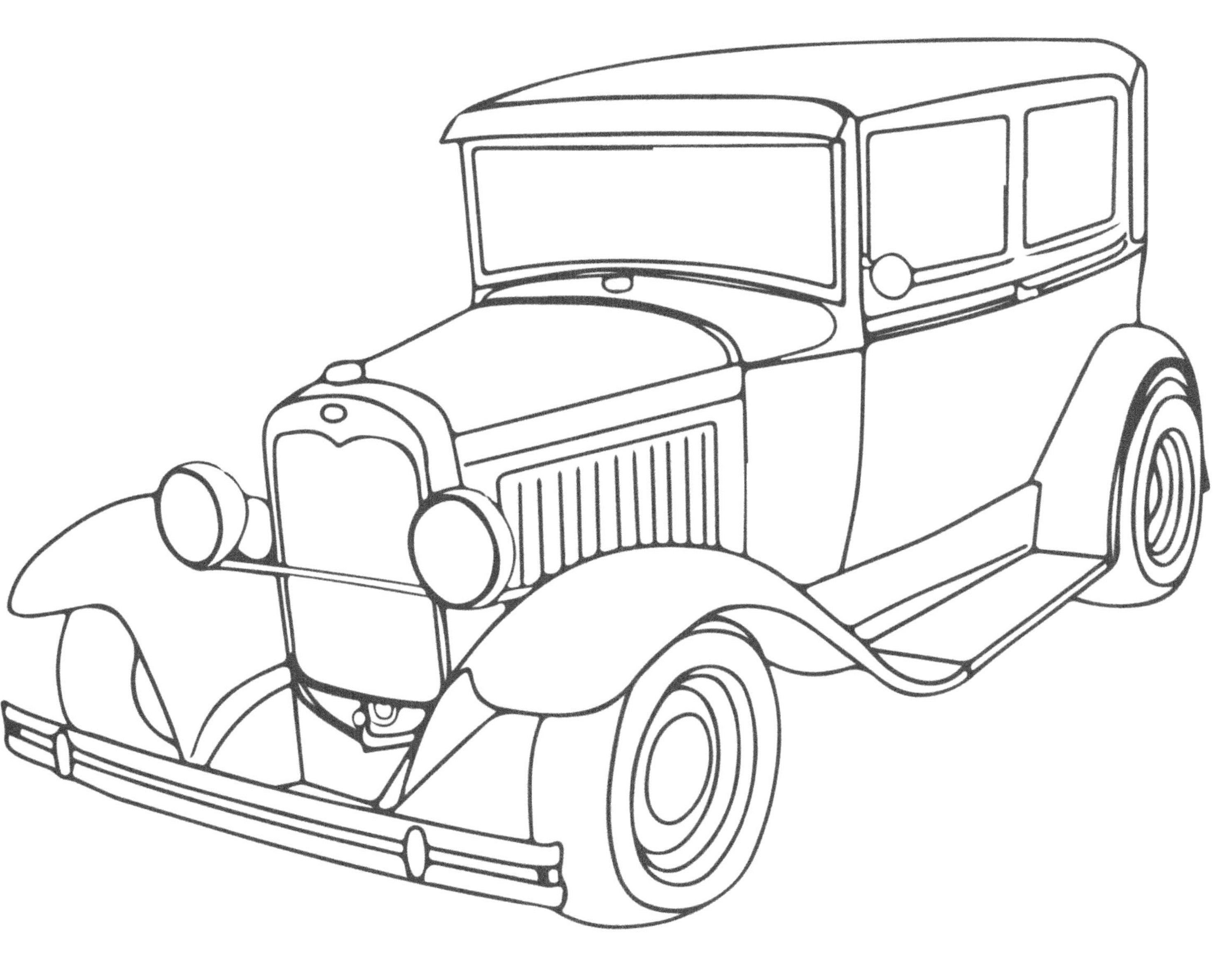

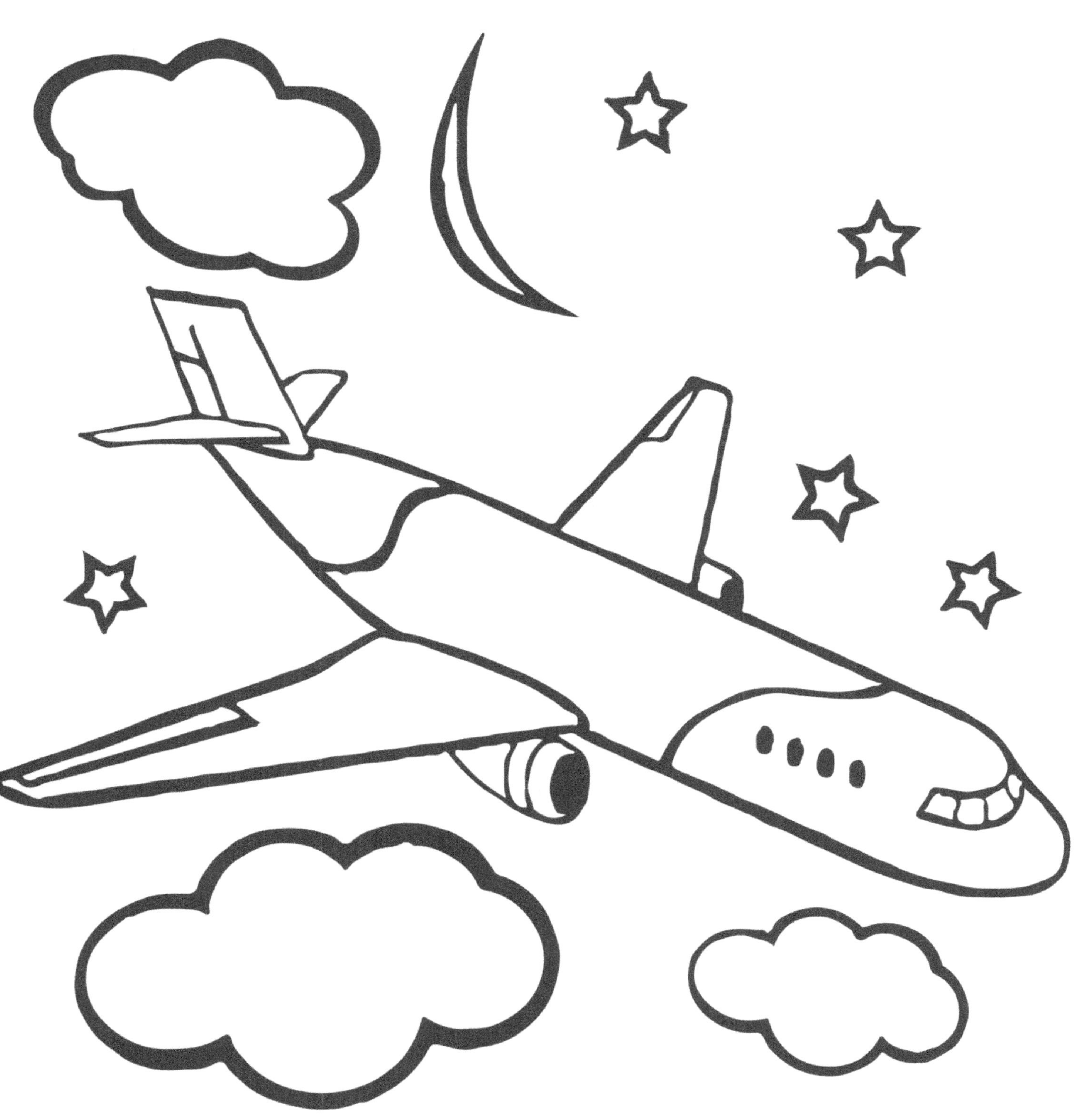

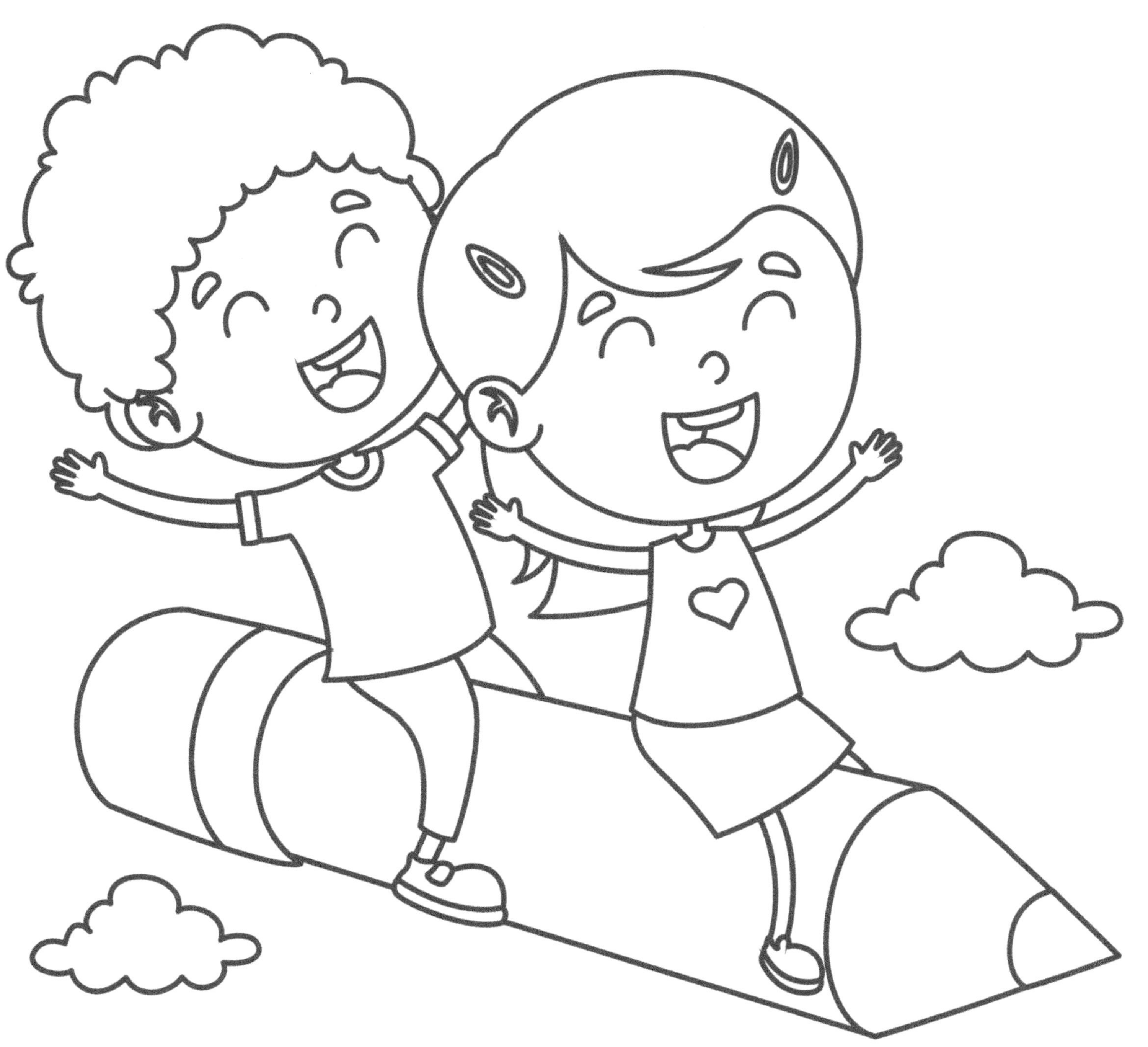

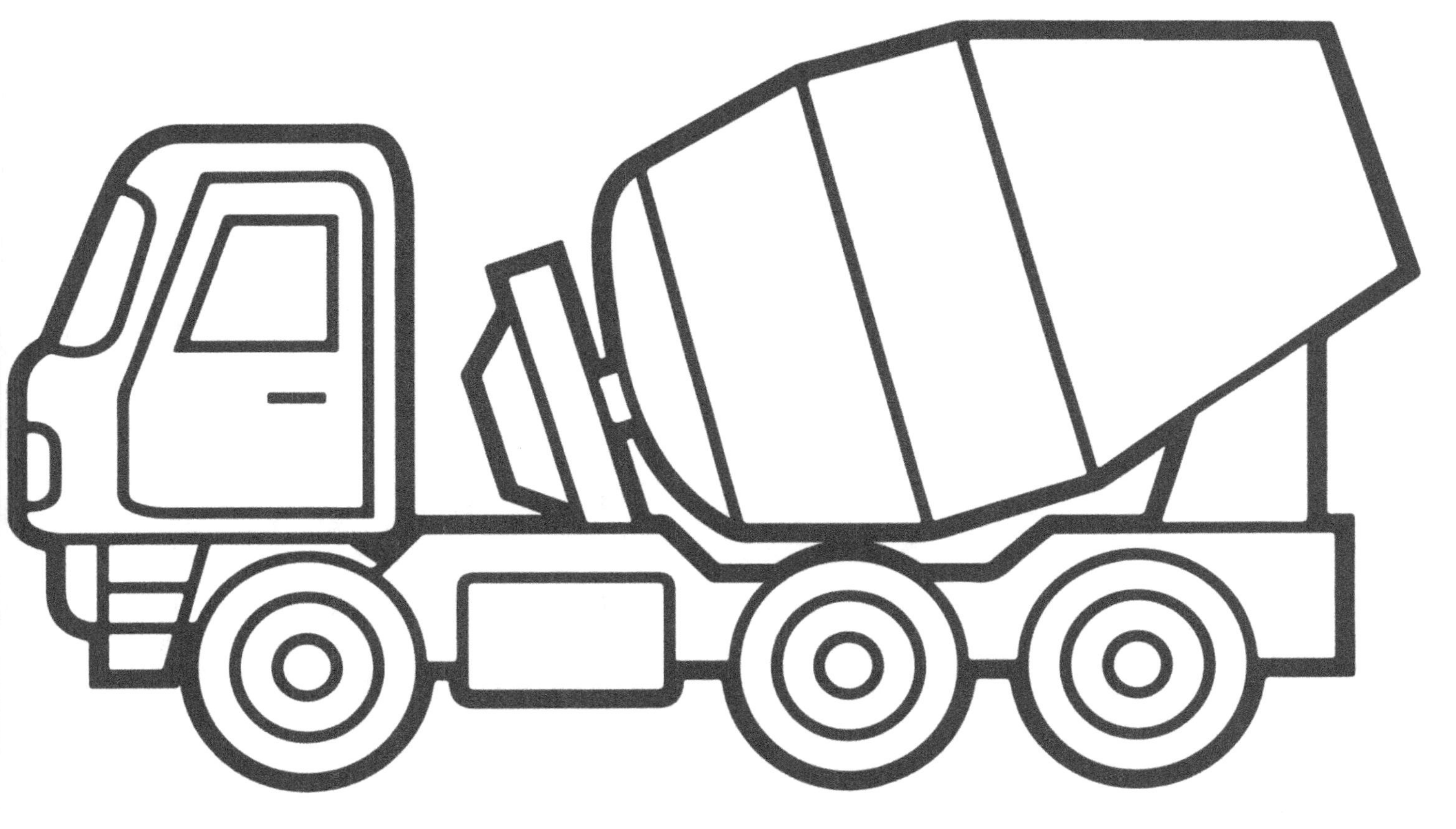

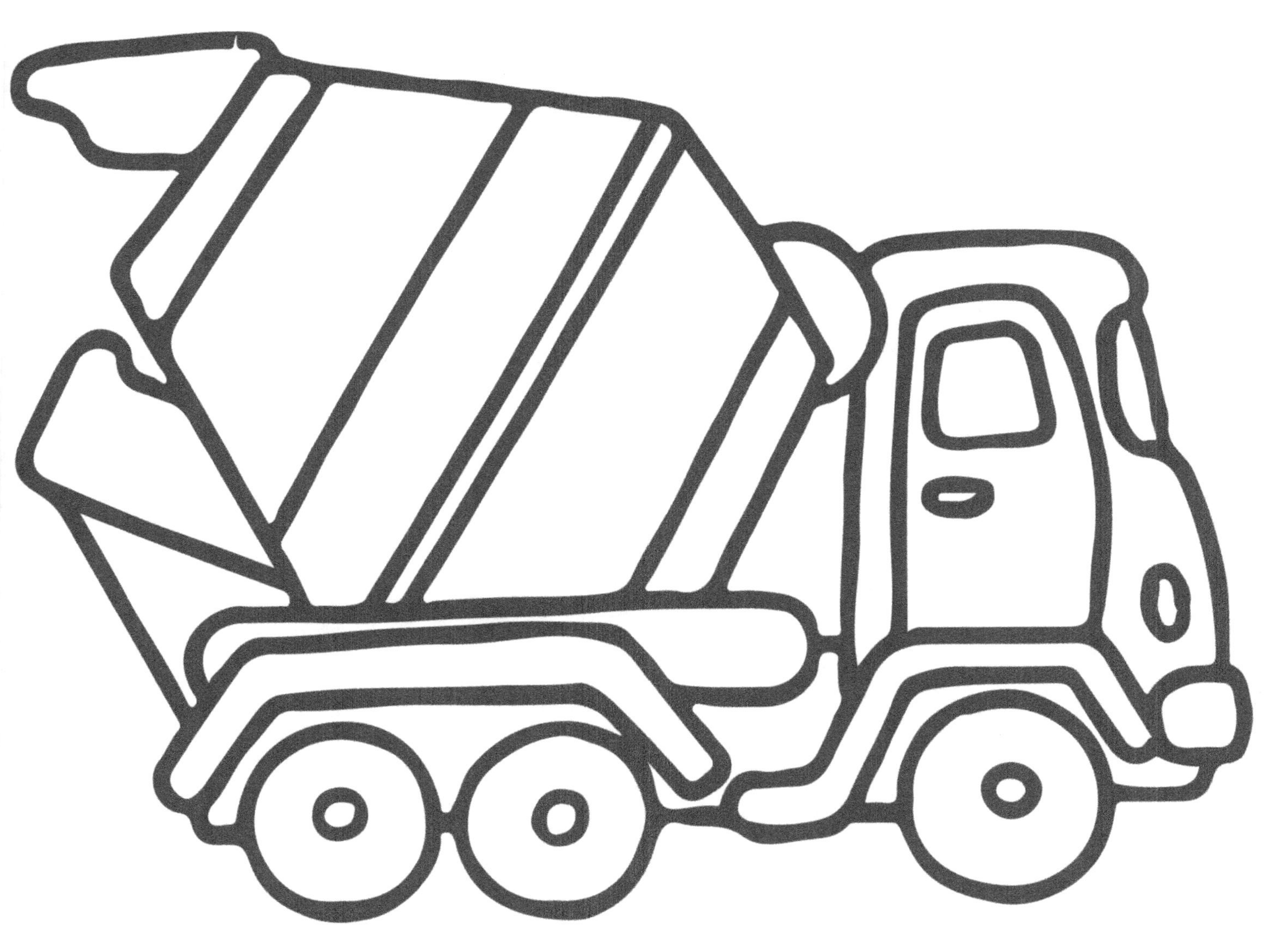

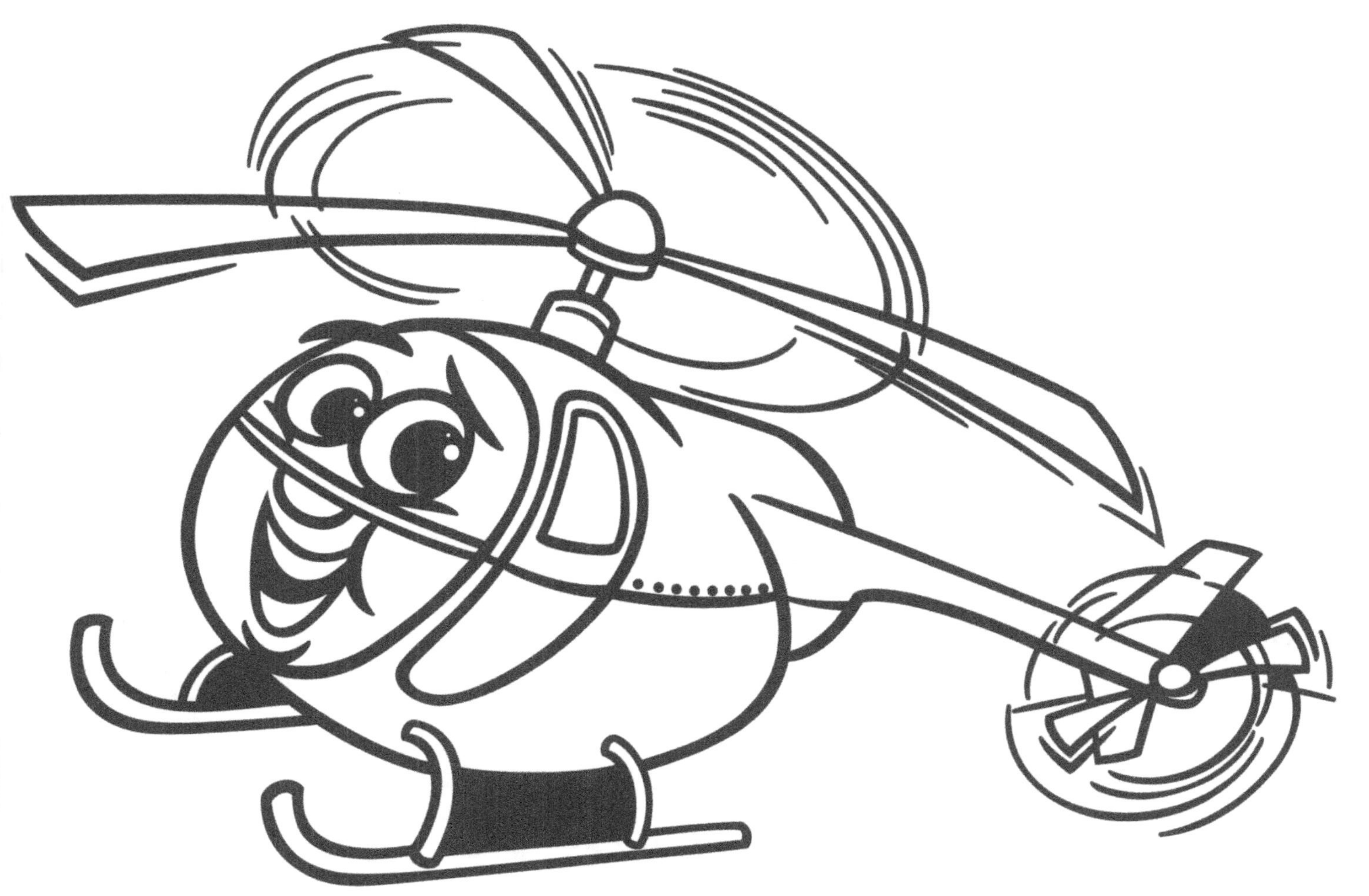

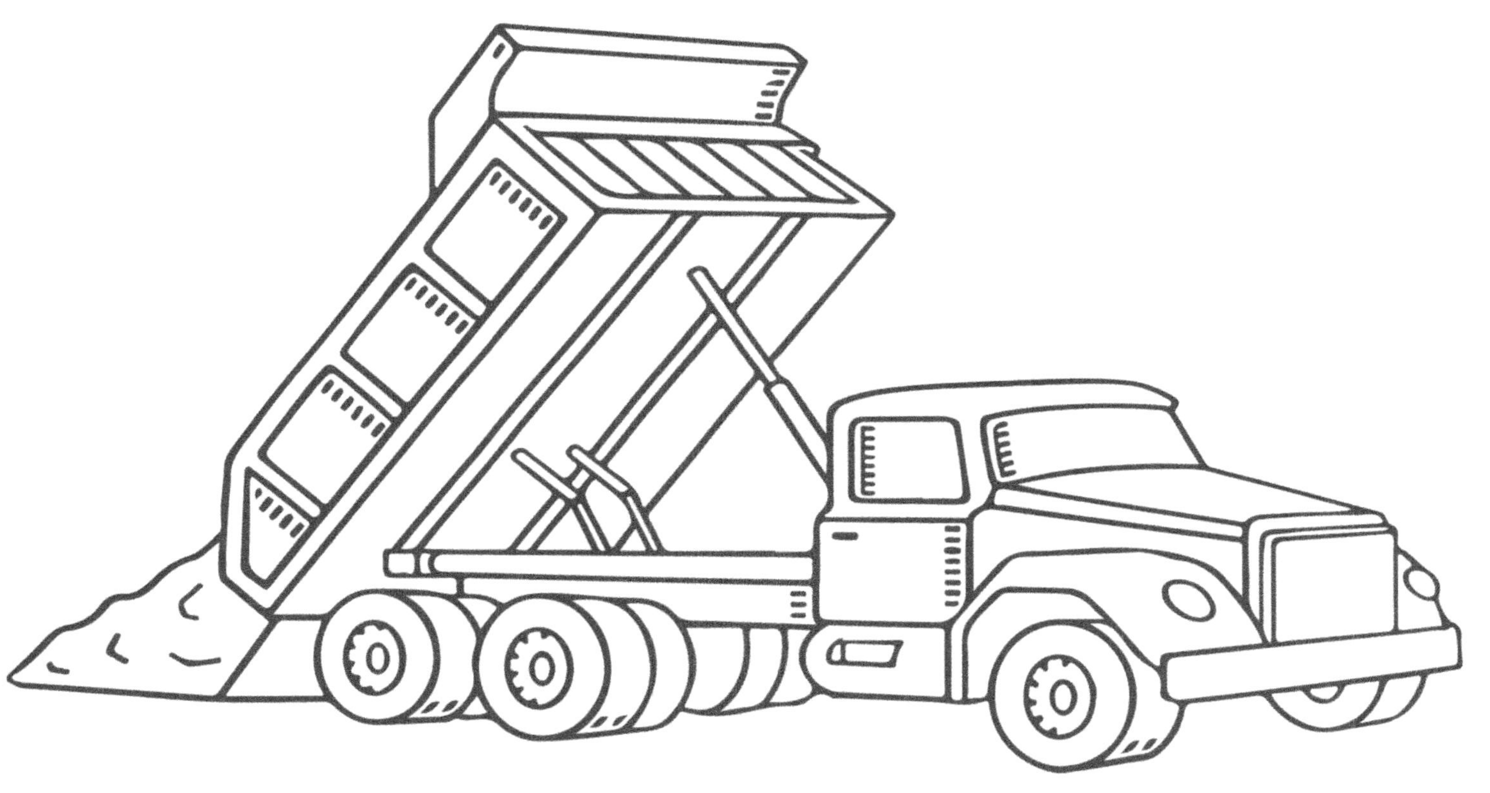

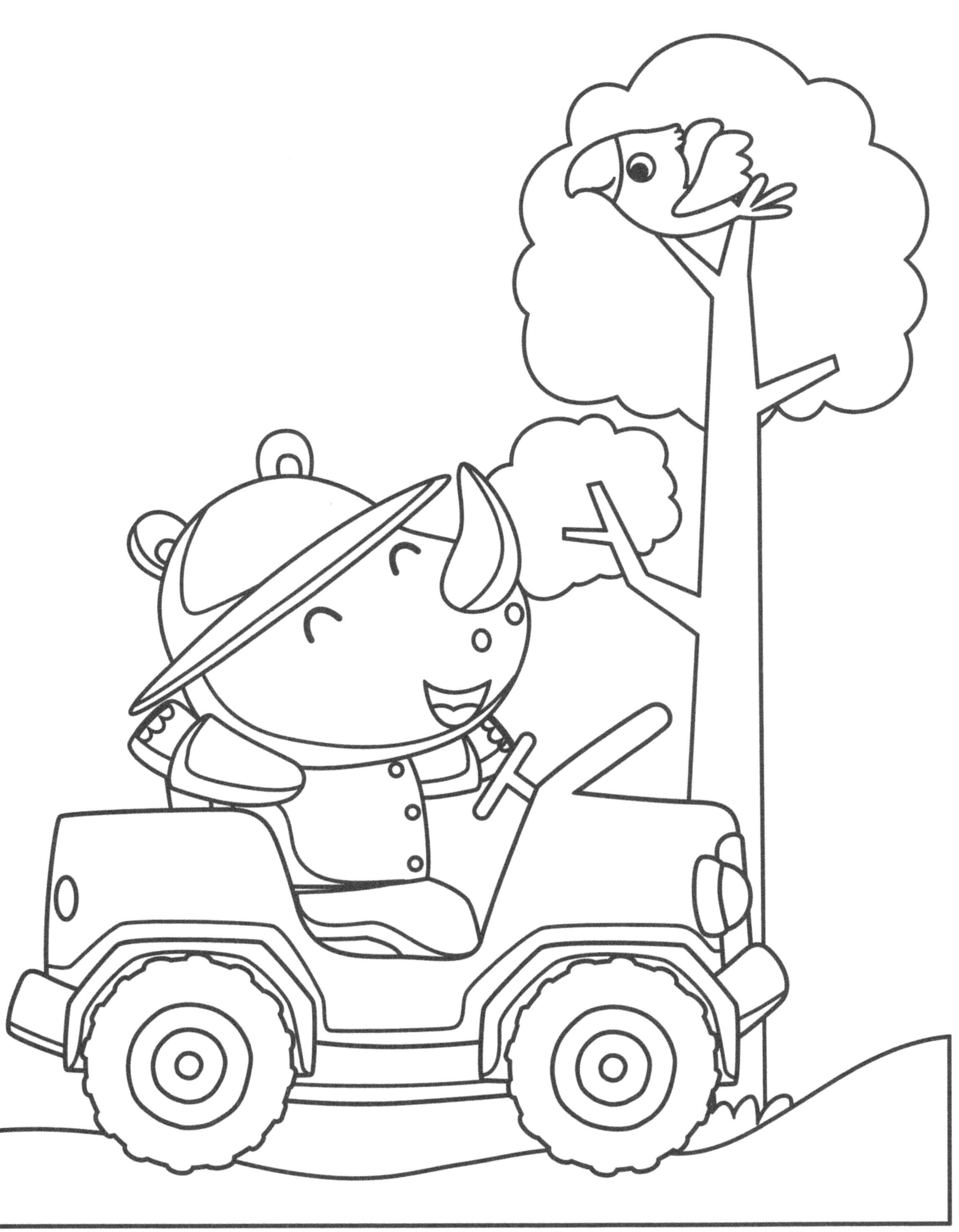

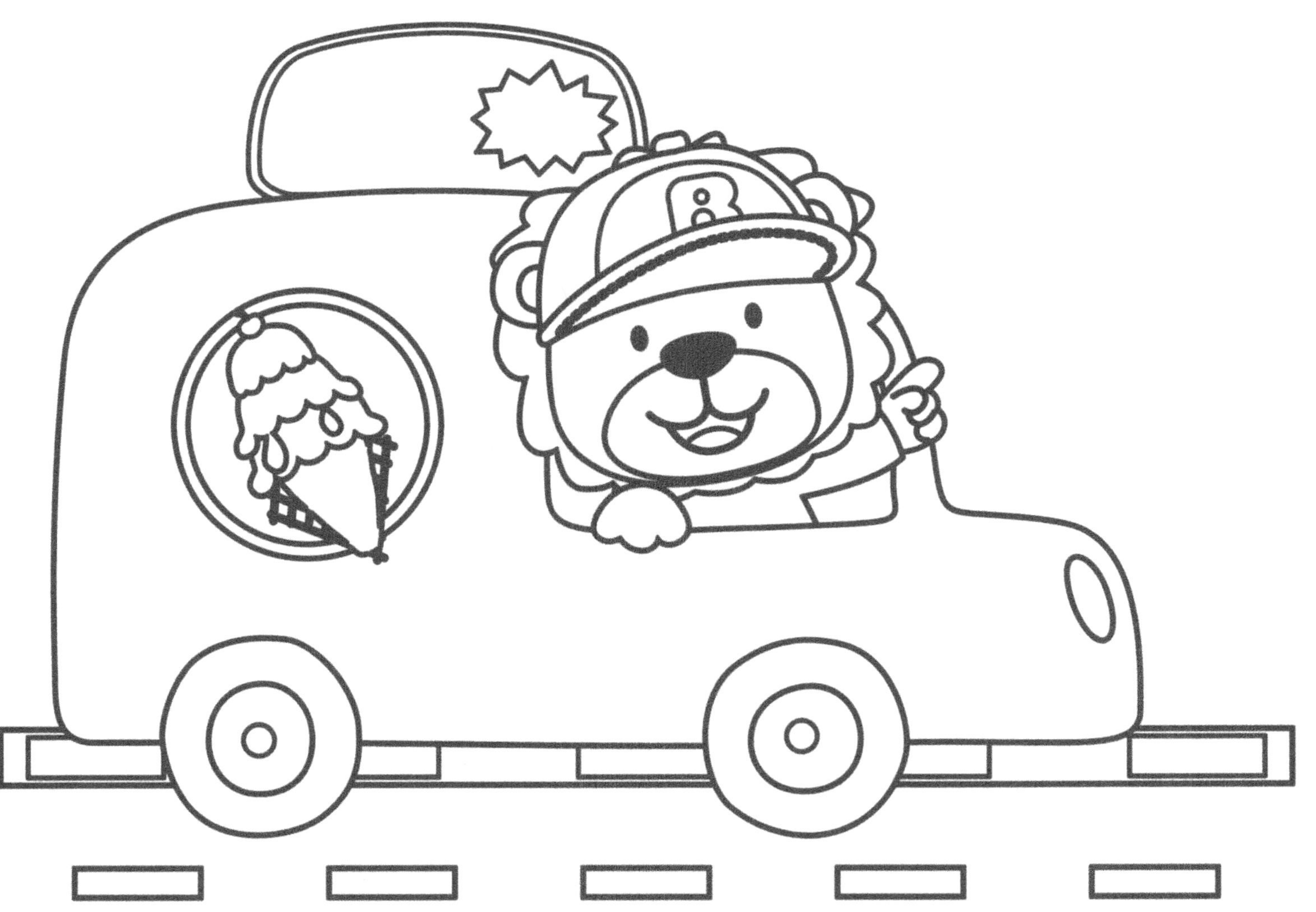

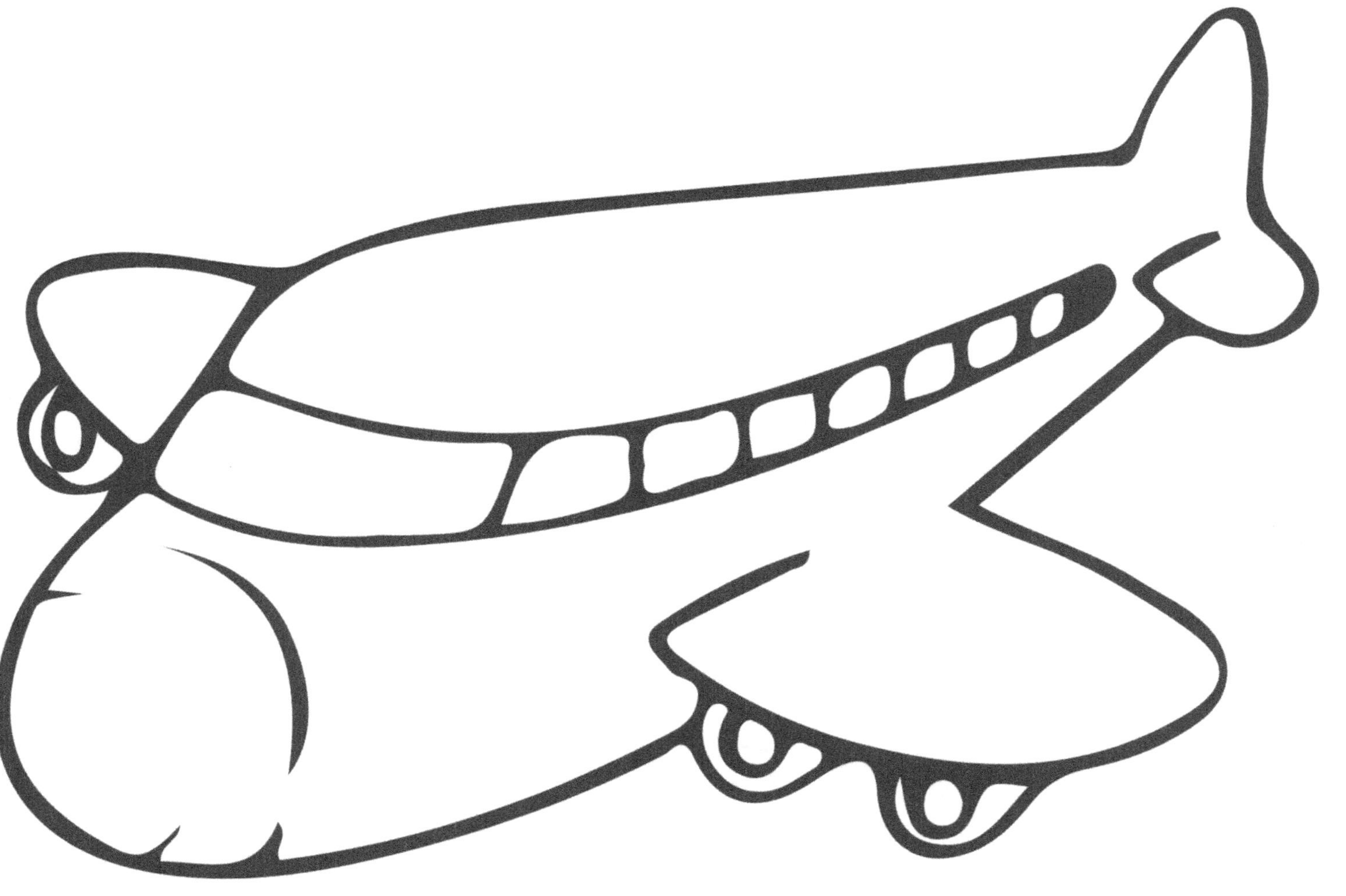

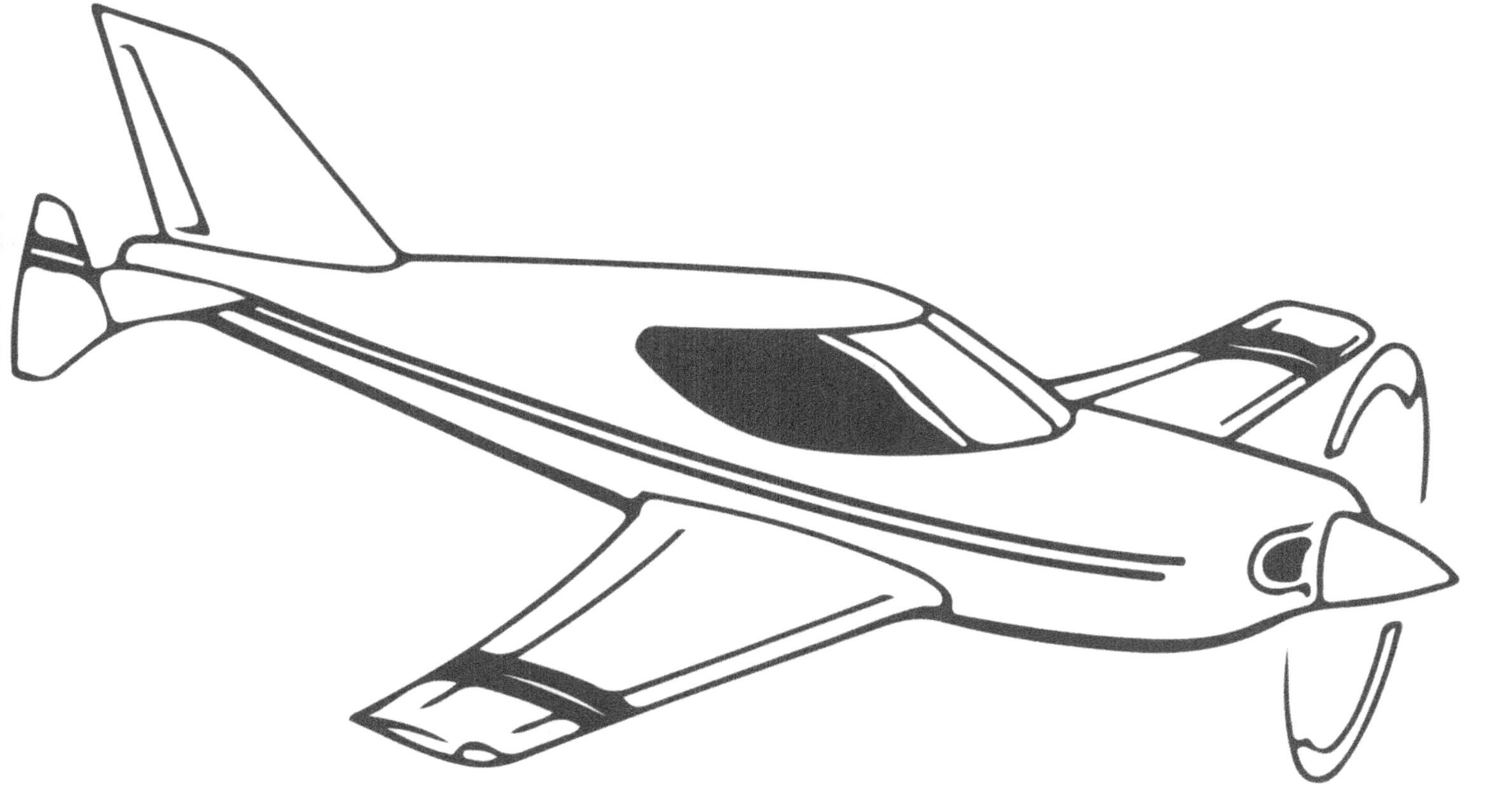

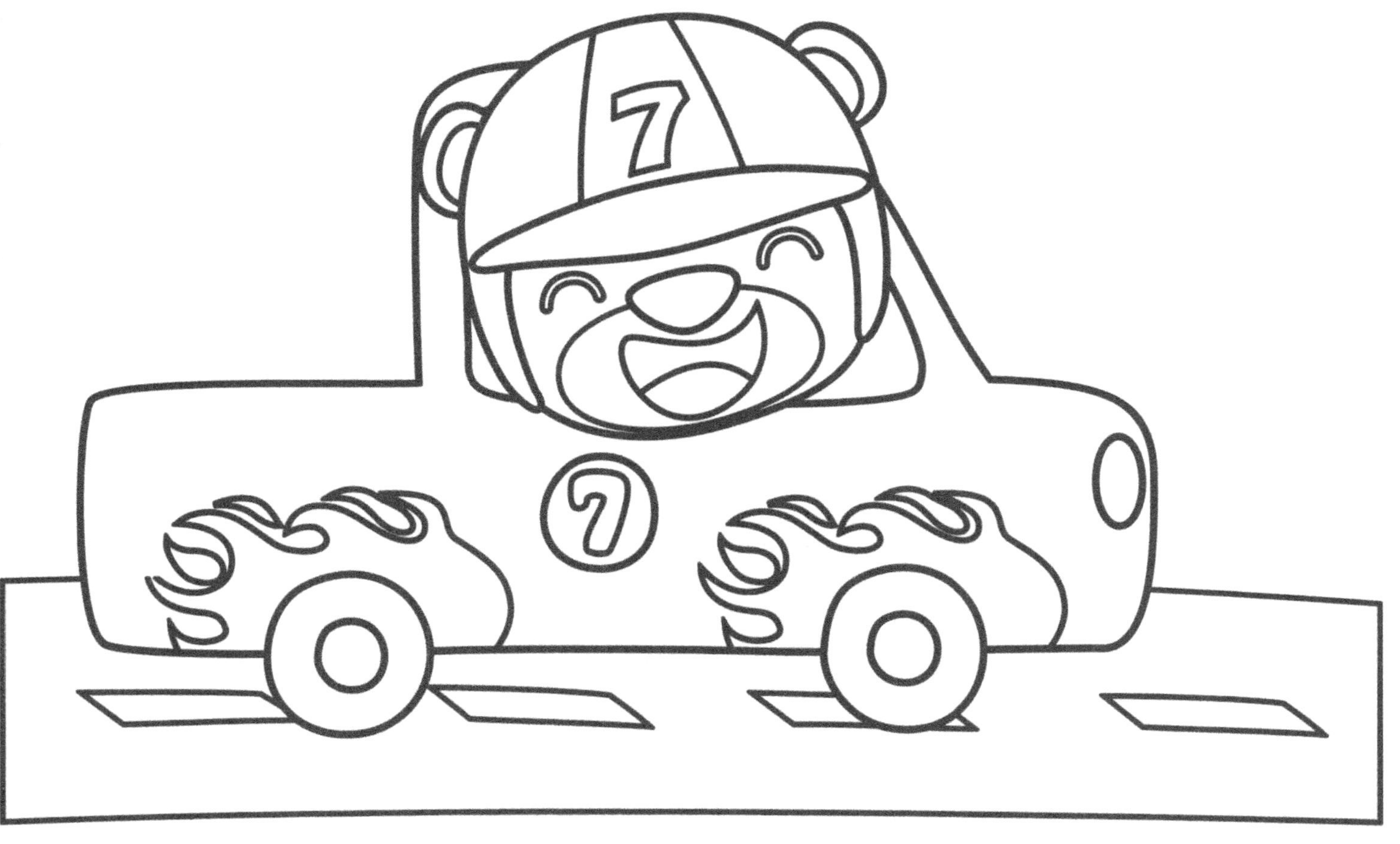

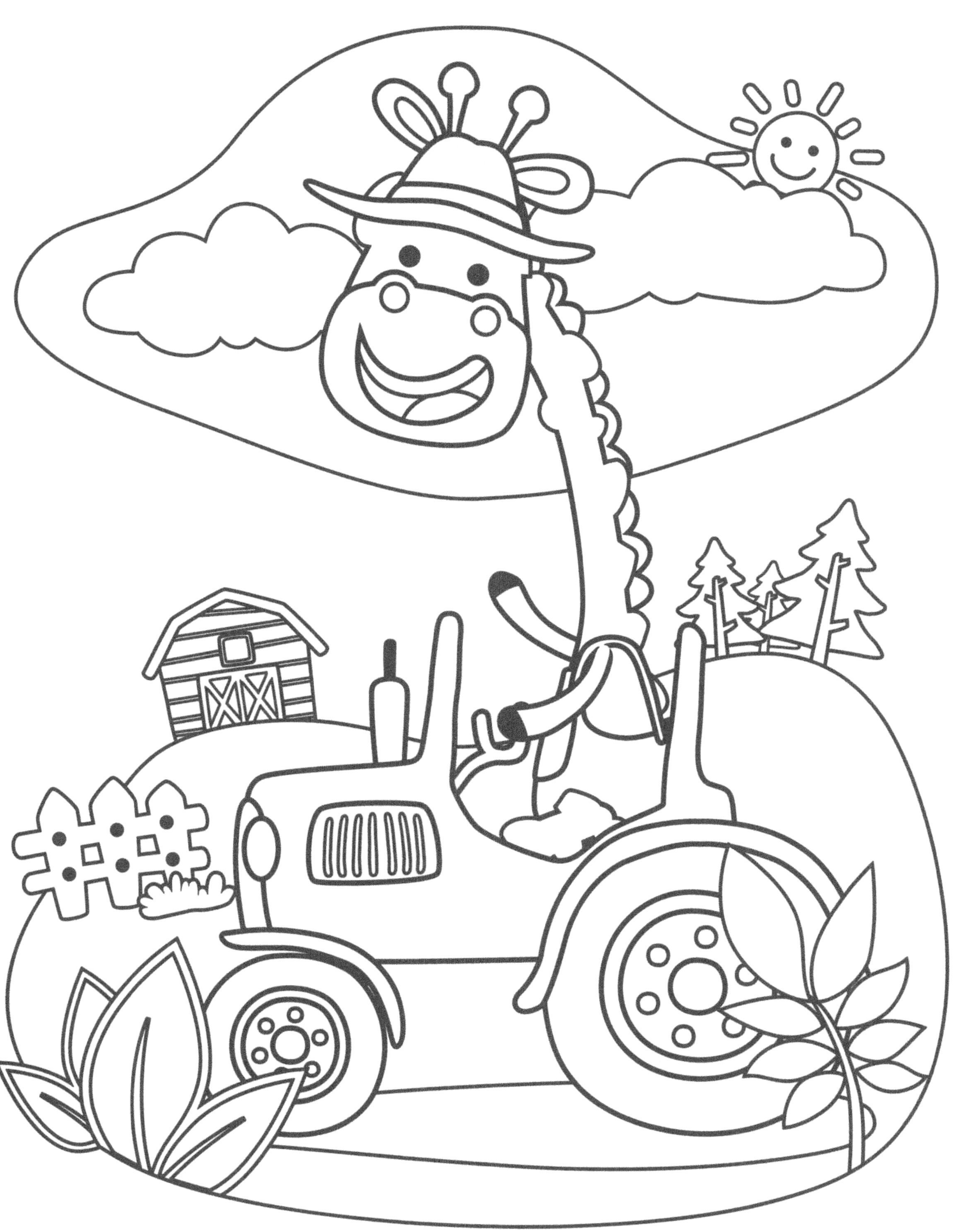

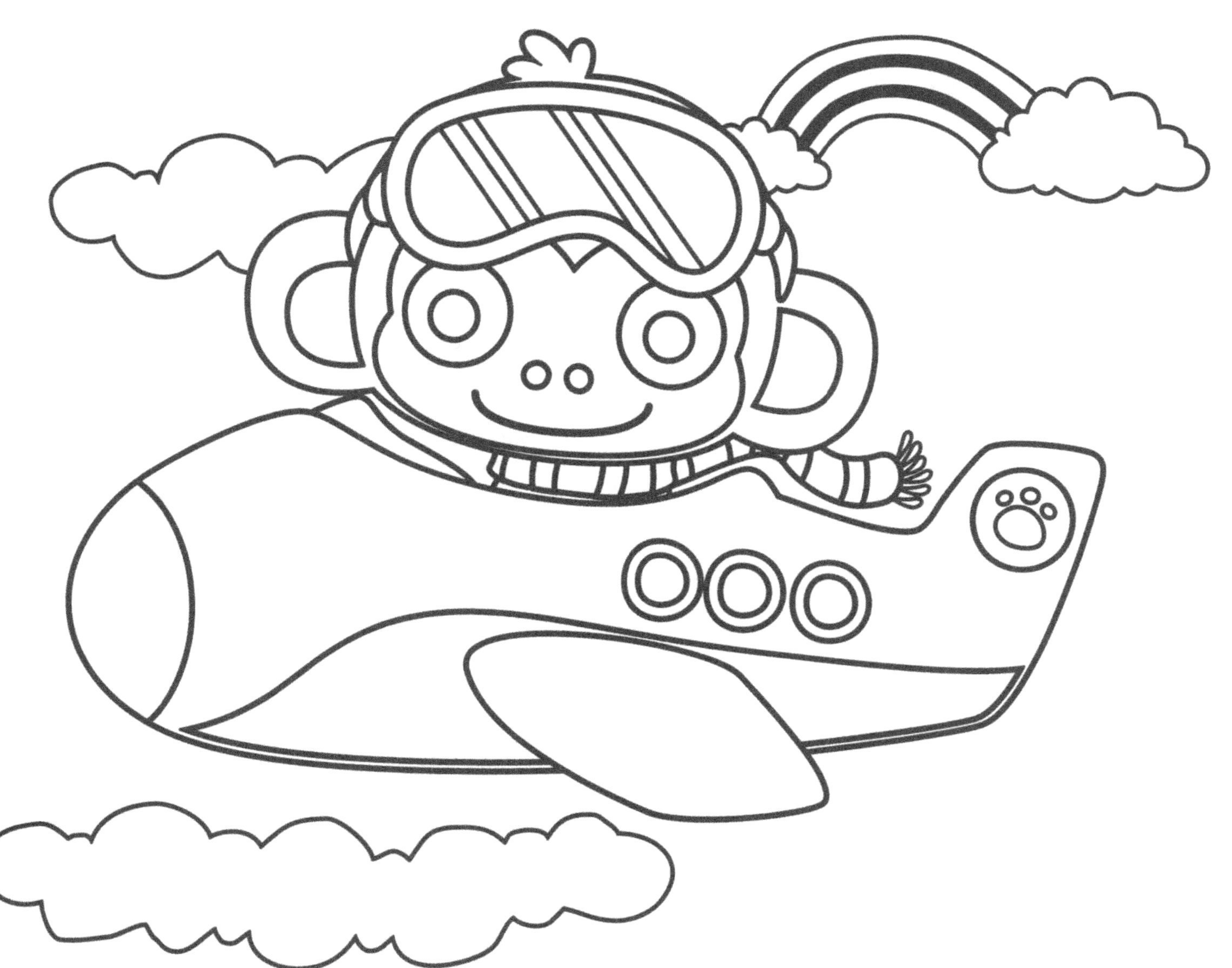

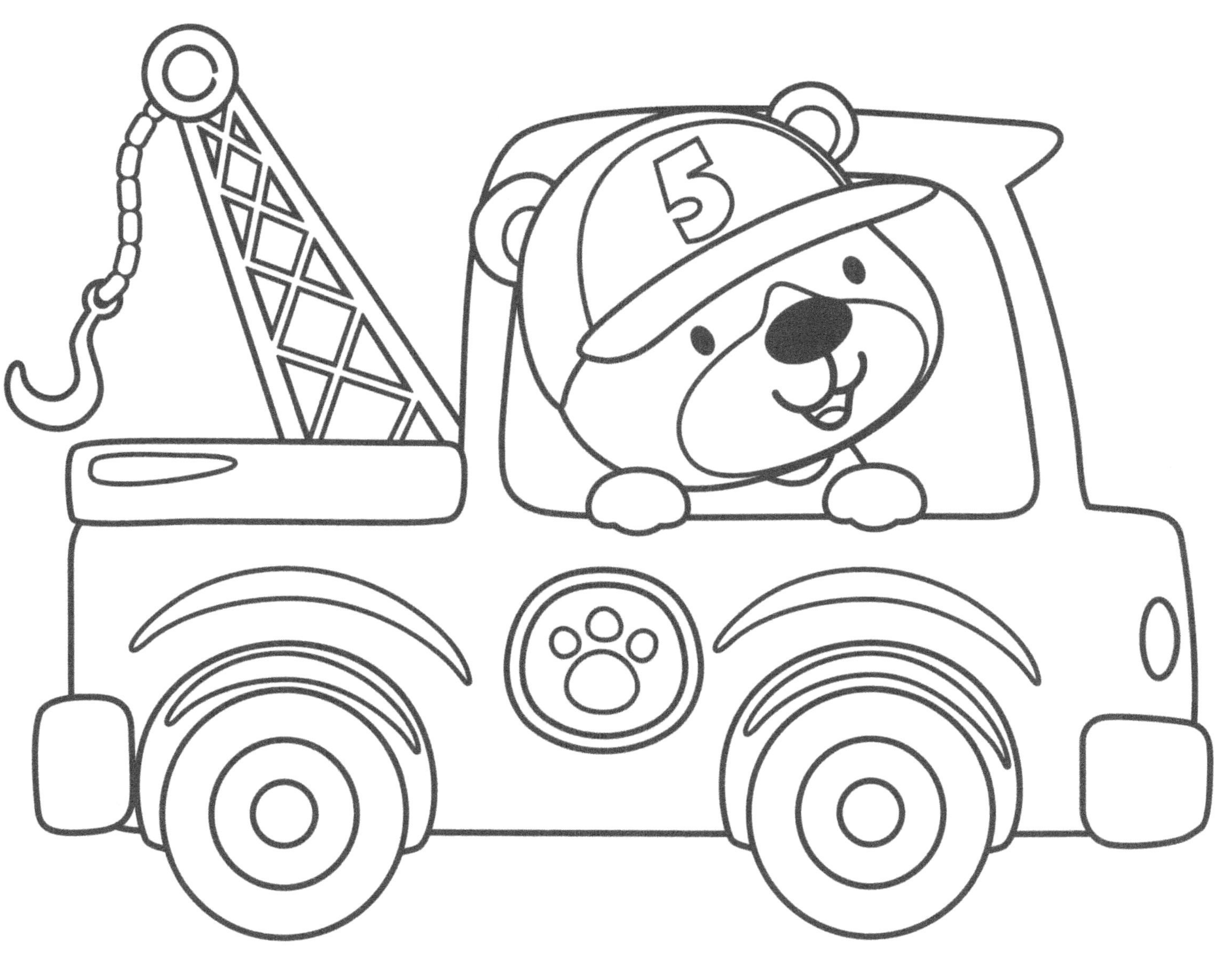

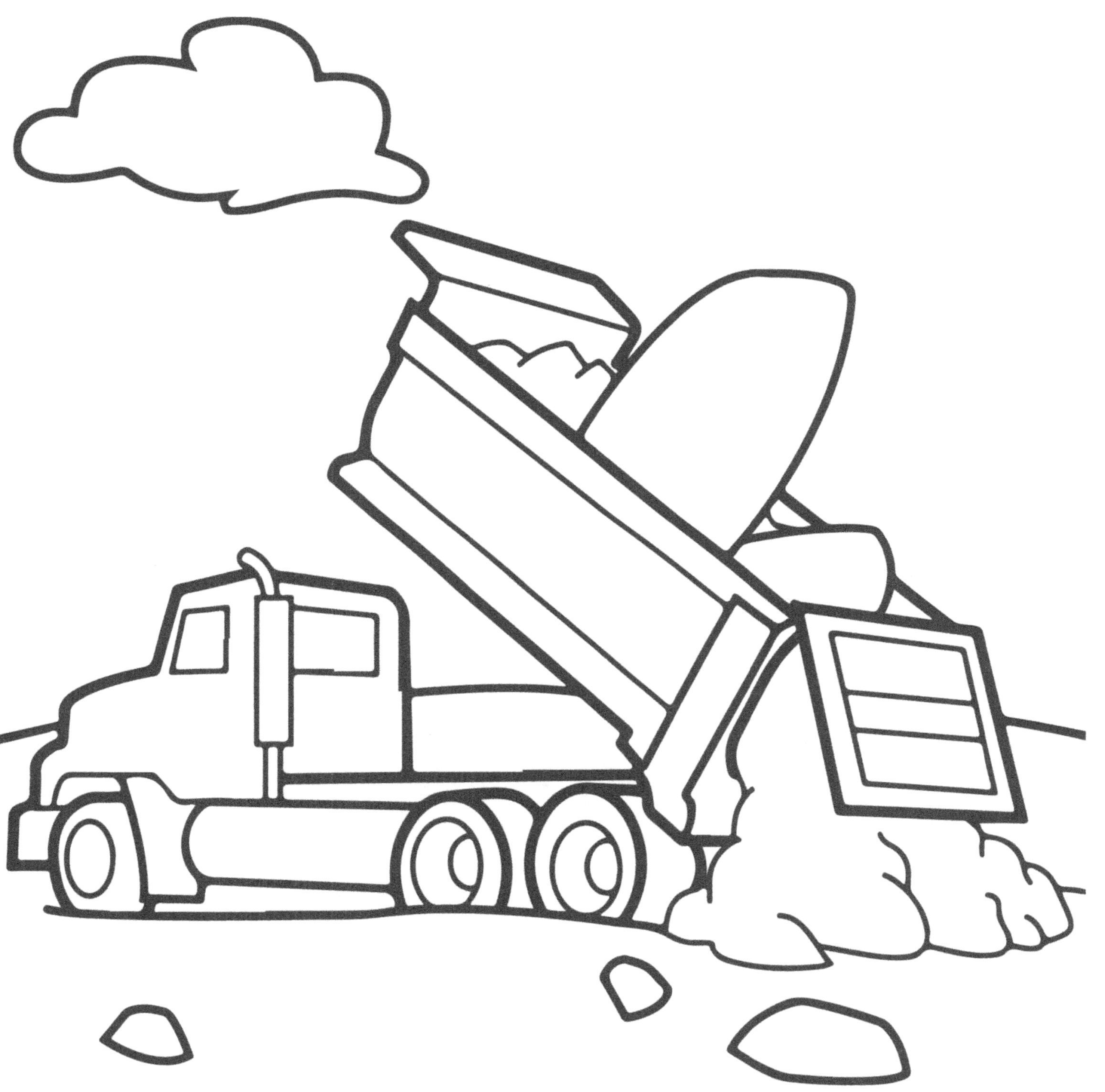

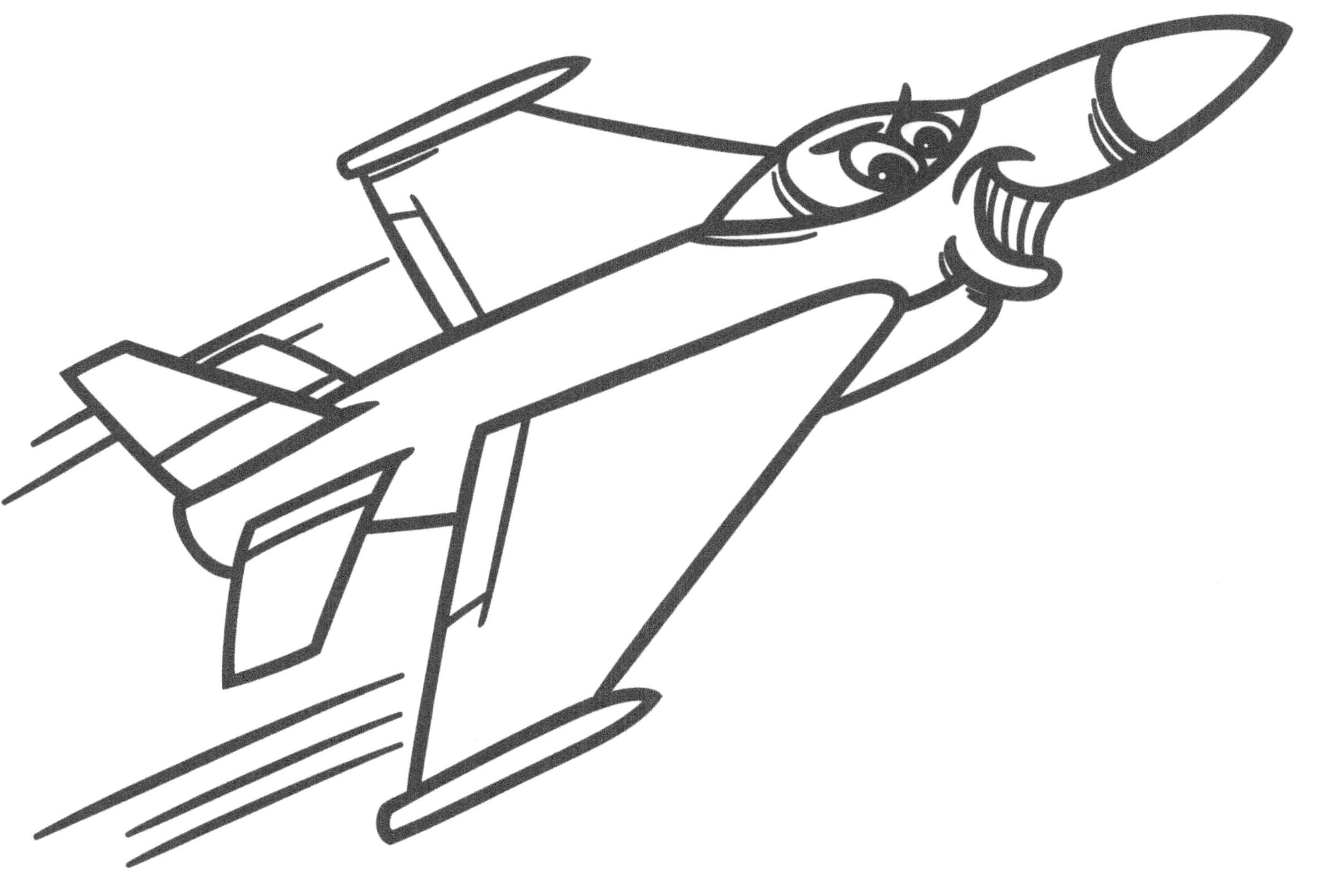

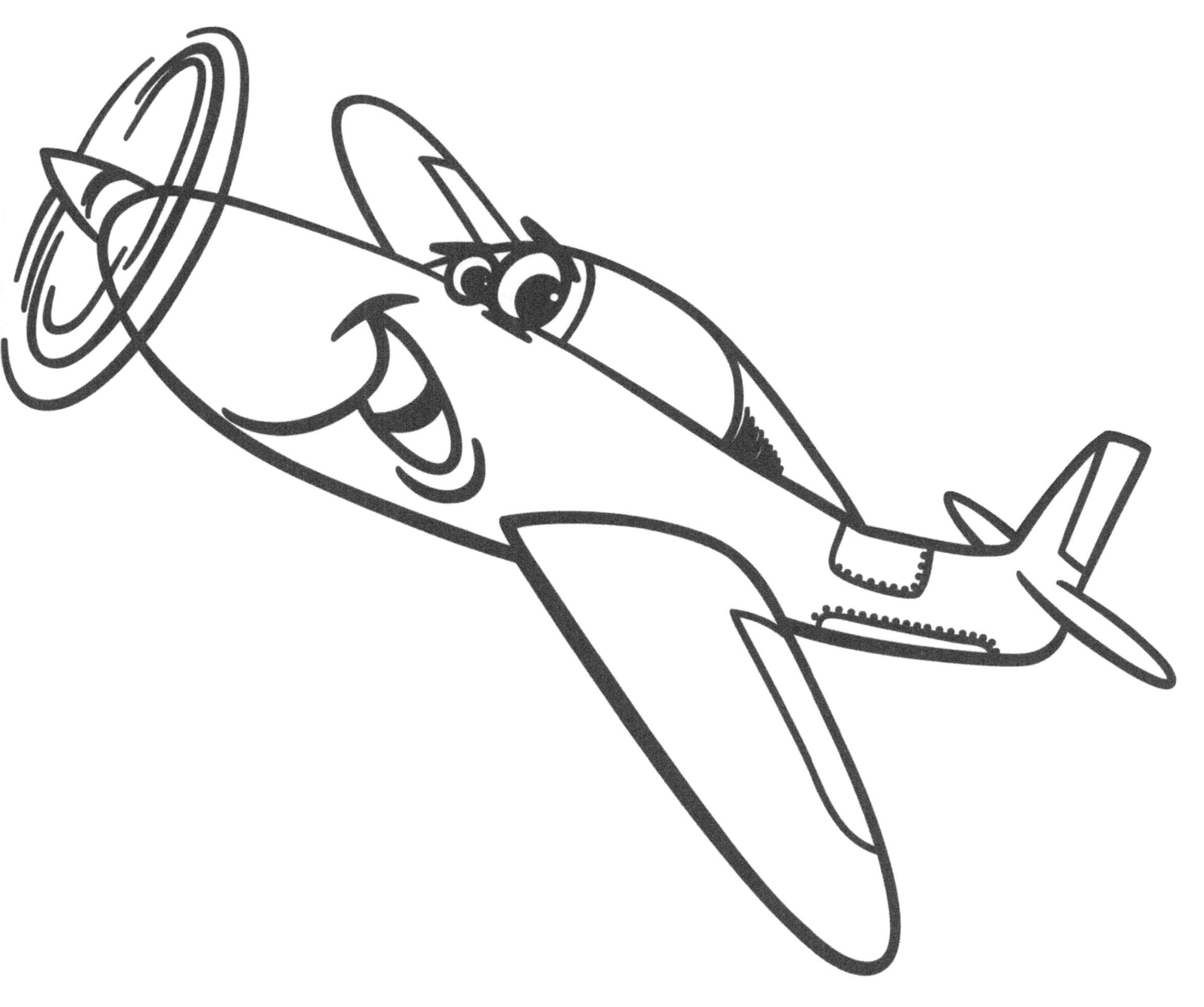

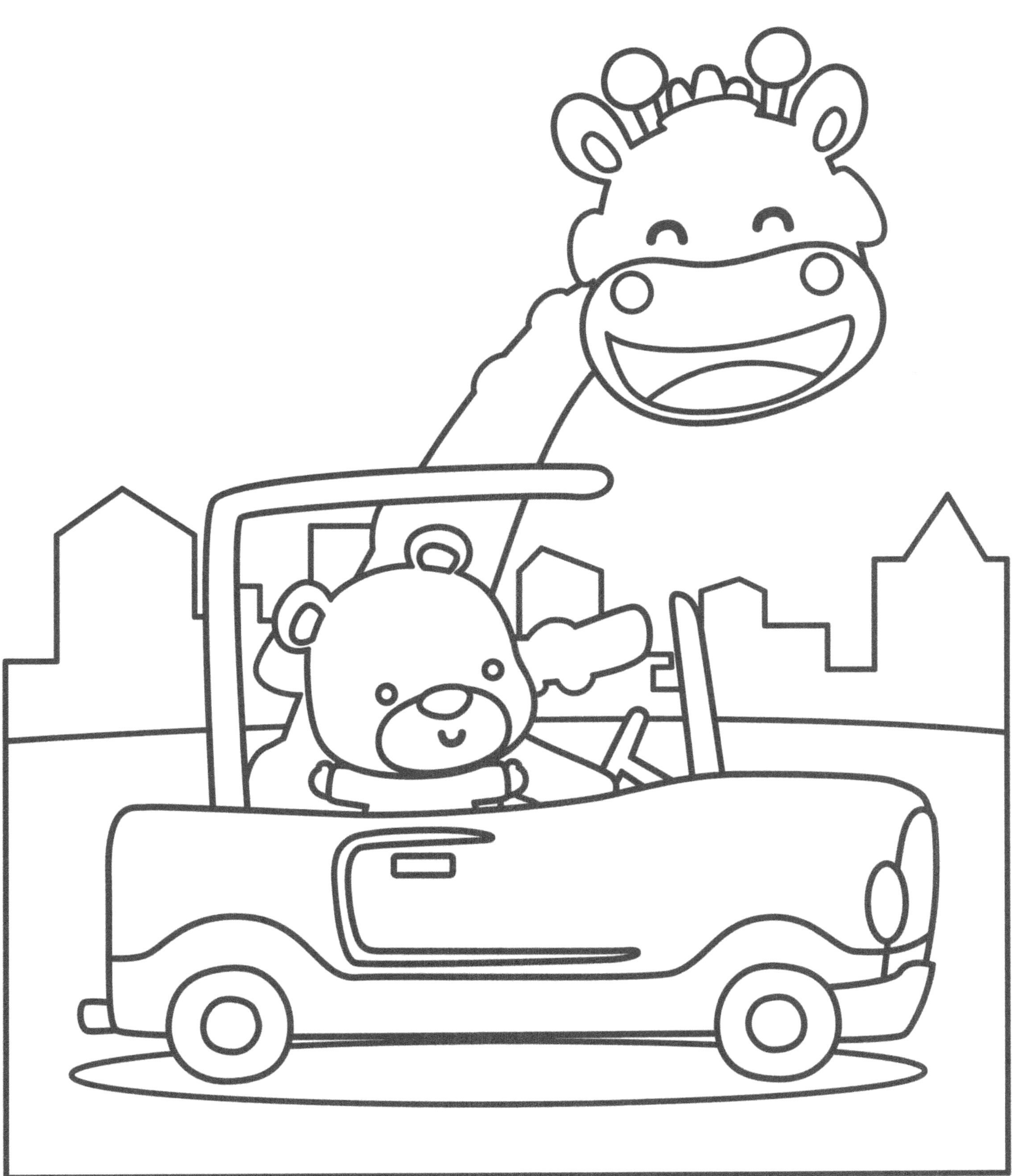

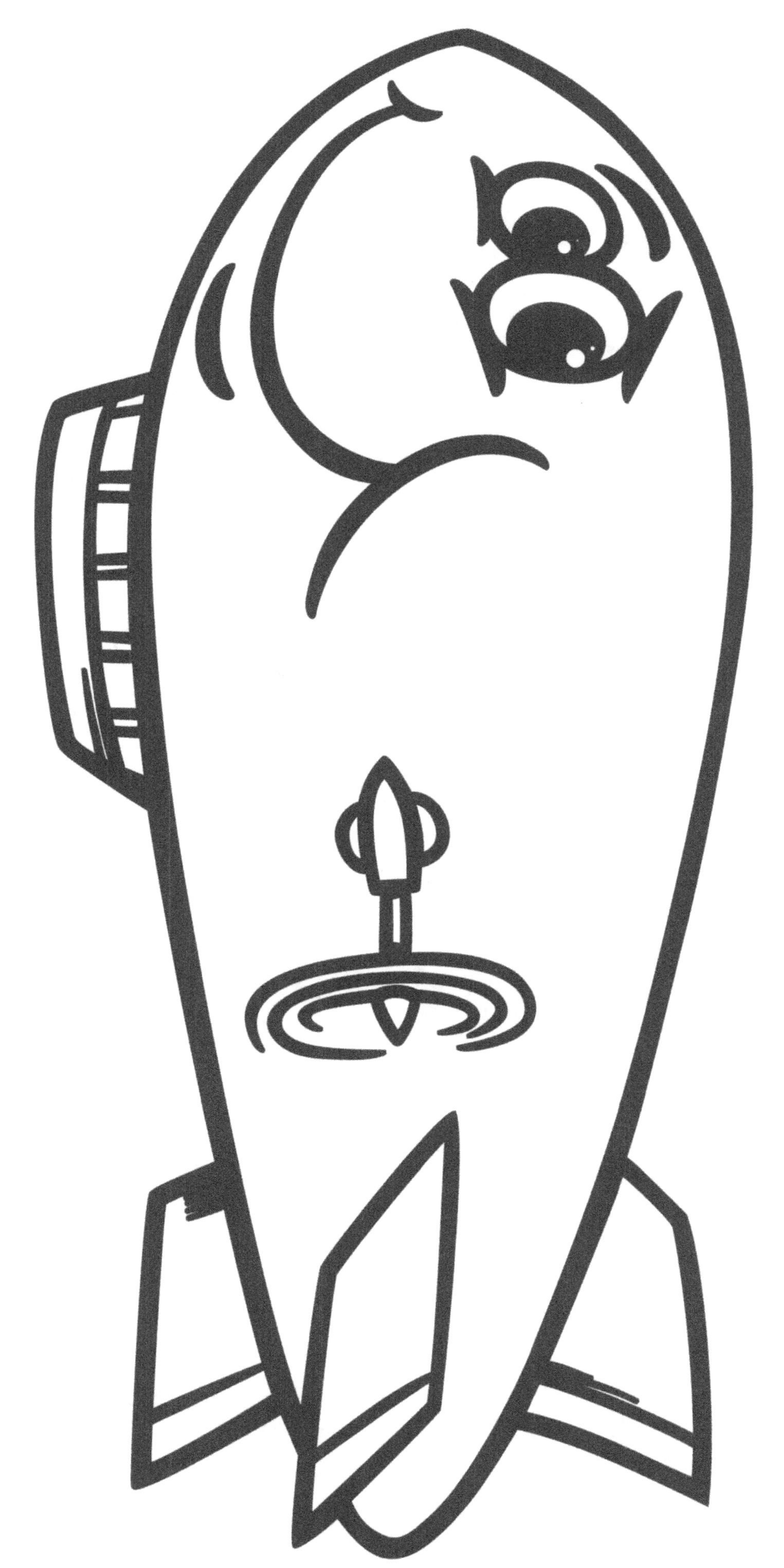

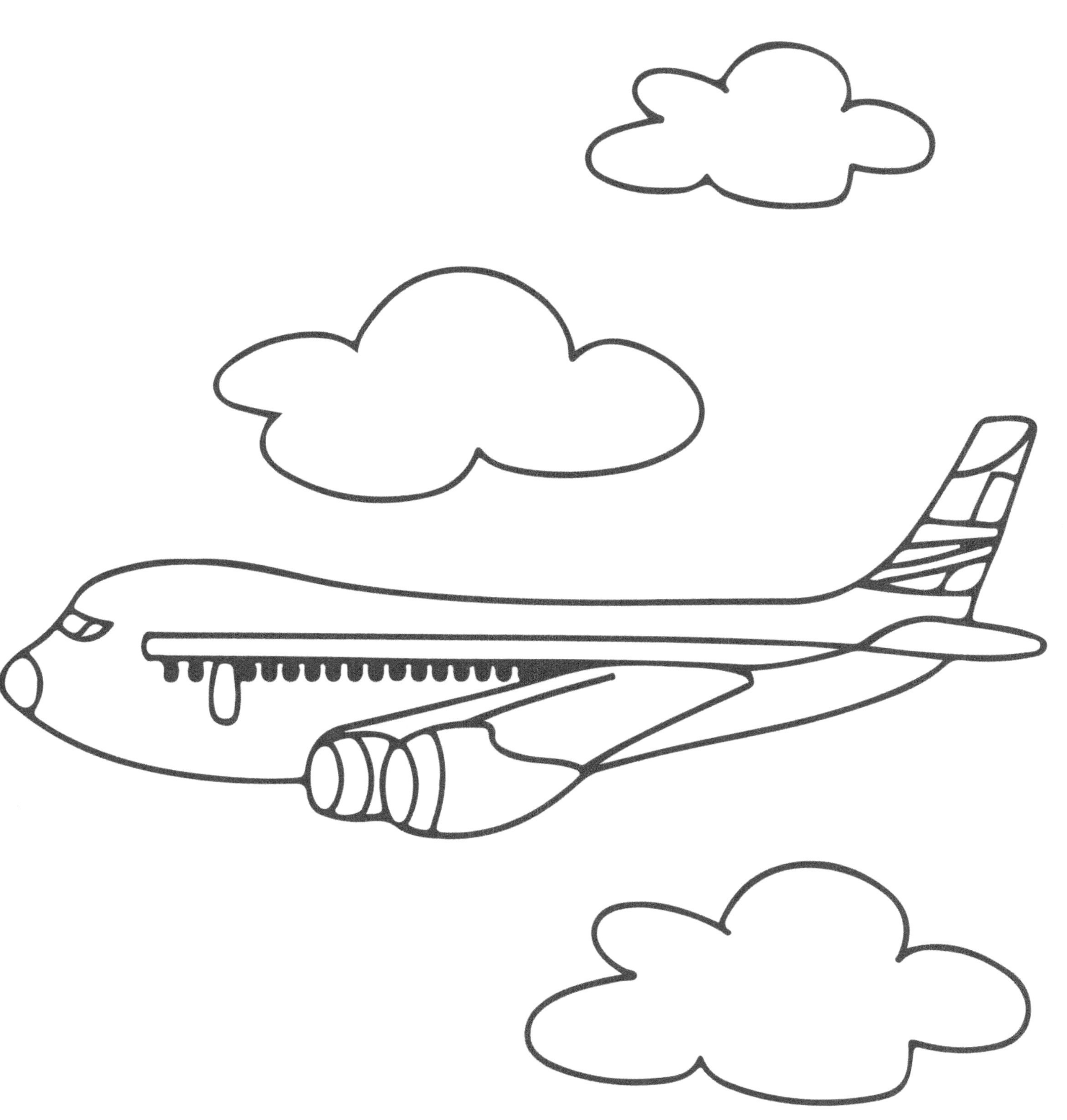